XAT²

Live Tax Free

The Really Important Book Company
London England

XAT [2]

is created by a friend who does not object to individuals making copies to share, asking they respect not to change it,

but maintains full copyright to prevent unauthorised mass production and resale.

The entire text is available to download free from:

www.xat.org

A Really Important Book

Published on licence from

Those Publishers, London England

by

The Really Important Book Company

P.O Box 25846 London N5 2GZ

Printed in Wales by yLolfa.

British Library Cataloguing in Publication Data

Publishers. Those XAT [2,] 1.

General Knowledge 1.

Title 615.4
362.1

082

ISBN see cover

File Under Pop Culture

Dedicated to You

Dear Reader,
All across the world people are
receiving copies of XAT
when they least expect it.

As you read on you will see
why this is happening.

You are meant to be here.

This is meant for you.

With Special Thanks to

Everyone who helped to make this possible

and thanks to

Bill Still

for historical quotes from his excellent program

"The Money Masters"

"In a Gentle Way
You Can Shift The World"

GANDHI

Part One
A Brief History of Money
(the past)

Part Two
The Model for a
Tax Free Economy
(the future)
starts page 45

Let's Go FORWARD

Most of us using money don't realise we are paying a hidden tax to a privately owned company for the privilege of having cash in our pockets. While using money has become a vital part of life, behind the scenes a system has been devised by a small elite group of people allowing them to profit from each and every transaction we make.

Because money affects almost every aspect of our lives, how it works is something we should all be interested in understanding further, however we are mostly discouraged from doing this by experts, who assure us the topic is much too complicated for most of us to grasp.

Our accepting this leaves the whole subject largely unexplored, and allows those who do know to carry on unquestioned. As a result it is estimated that only one person in a thousand actually understands how money is created.

XAT comes in two simple parts. The first part exposing how our unfair financial system came into being, and the second part exploring how a fair system of trade could easily take its place, if enough of us wanted that.

The history section confirms in many ways that the futuristic ideas are sound. Some of you who are already aware of historical trends might find it more entertaining to read the second part first, and then look back at the examples we have selected to base our conclusions on. You'll also find a section at the end which allows you to ask questions and suggest things you feel should be included in future editions.

Reading it will not make you a financial wizard, but it will make you a 'one in a thousand' and hopefully in time help to raise the odds in favour of a better world.

Far from being just entertaining information, this should leave you with the desire to withdraw your support from the present unfair system, and begin something new. To satisfy this natural desire we include some suggestions: but first lets see how it was done.

To understand how money is created and how this could change, read on....

"History records that the money changers have used every form of abuse, intrigue, deceit, and violent means possible to maintain their control over governments by controlling money and its issuance."
President James Madison

Money, money, money, it's always just been there, right? Wrong.

Obviously it's issued by the government to make it easy for us to exchange things. Wrong again!

Truth is that most people don't realise that the issuing of money is a private business, and that the privilege of issuing money has been a major bone of contention throughout history.

Wars have been fought and depressions have been caused in the battle over who issues the money. The majority of people are not aware of this because the current winners of this battle control the media and what is taught in school.

You might find some of this hard to believe and many will be shocked by what they read, but it's important to say here that this first section is genuine history backed by quotes which anyone can verify if they have a mind to.

While we might feel powerless in trying to stop the manipulation of money for private profit at our expense, it is easy to forget that we collectively give money its value. We have been taught to believe printed pieces of paper have special value, and because we know others believe this too, we are willing to work all our lives to get what we are convinced others will want.

An honest look at history will show us how our innocent trust has been abused

Let's start our exploration of money with:

THE ROMAN EMPIRE (200 B.C. - 400 A.D.)

Once money is accepted as a form of exchange, those who produce, loan out and manipulate the quantity of money are obviously in a very strong position. They are the **"Money Changers"**.

Those who think that it has always been the government who controls the money might be surprised to learn that two early Roman Emperors reformed the Usury Laws of their time, limiting land ownership to five hundred acres. This was an attempt to diminish the power of the money changers who were working their trade quite independent from Caesar.

Both these Emperors were assasinated for their efforts.

Not one to be put off, in 48 B.C. Julius Caesar took back the power to make coins from the money changers and minted his own coins for the benefit of all the people.

He then proceeded to build many great public works with his new supply of plentiful money, and he became very popular with the common people.

The money changers were out of a job, but not for long. His assasination put them back in business.

After his death, money again was in short supply, being reduced by a whopping 90% and causing many to lose their homes.

Taxes increased with corruption bringing more usury and lower value coins, causing the Roman government loss of confidence, and loss of support from the masses. Rome was plunged into the gloom of the dark ages.

A bad time was had by all you might think, but that was not so.

As hard as it might be to believe, in times of economic upheaval, wealth is never destroyed but only transferred. And who benefits the most when money is scarce? You may have guessed. It's those controlling what everyone else wants, the money changers.

When the majority of people are suffering through economic depression, you can be sure that a minority of people are getting rich.

Let's have a look at what caused the coins to fly and brought the money changers to their knees to pick them up in 33 A.D.

JESUS FLIPS (many coins)

Jesus was so upset by the sight of the money changers in the temple, he waded in and started to tip over the tables and drive them out with a whip, this being the only time we hear of him using force during his entire ministry.

So what were the money changers doing there in the first place?

The Jews were called upon to pay their temple tax with a special coin called the half shekel. It was a measured half ounce of pure silver with no image of a pagan emperor on it.

It was to them the only coin acceptable to God.

Because there was only a limited number of these coins in circulation, the money changers were in a buyer's market, and as with anything else in short supply, they were able to raise the price to what the market would bare.

They made huge profits with their monopoly on these coins and turned this time of devotion into a mockery for profit. Jesus saw this as stealing from the people and proclaimed the whole setup to be. "A den of thieves".

This incident might have been part of what prompted Saint Paul to later say his famous, often misquoted line. "The love of money is the root of all evil"

Moving forward in time by a thousand years, things are no better in:

MEDIEVAL ENGLAND (1000 - 1100 A.D.)

Here we find goldsmiths offering to keep other people's gold and silver safe in their vaults, and people walking away with a receipt for what they have left there. The paper receipts became popular for trade because they were less heavy to carry around than gold and silver coins.

One day, after a while, a goldsmith must have noticed that only a small percentage of the depositors ever came in to demand their gold at any one time, so he made out some receipts for gold *which wasn't there* and loaned it out to make more interest.

He must have told a few of his goldsmith friends, because soon they were all doing it. With a nod and a wink among themselves, they incorporated this practice into the banking system. They even gave it a name to make it seem more acceptable, christening the practice "Fractional Reserve Banking" which translates to mean, lending out many times more money than you have assets on deposit.

Today banks are allowed to loan out at least ten times the amount they actually are holding, so while you wonder how they get rich charging you 11% interest, it's not 11% a year they make on that amount but actually 110%.

Move forward 100 years and we find King Henry the First working on a way to pull the power away from the money changers hands yet again.

THE TALLY STICKS (1100 - 1854)

King Henry the First produced sticks of polished wood, with notches cut along one edge to signify the denominations. The stick was then split full length so each piece still had a record of the notches.

The King kept one half for proof against counterfeiting, and then spent the other half into the market place where it would circulate as money.

Because only Tally Sticks were accepted by Henry for payment of taxes, there was a built in demand for them, which gave people confidence to accept these as money.

He could have used anything really, so long as the people agreed it had value, and his willingness to accept these sticks as legal tender made it easy for the people to agree. **Money is only as valuable as people's faith in it, and without that faith even today's money is just paper.**

The tally stick system worked really well for 726 years. It was the most successful form of currency in recent history and the British Empire was actually built under the Tally Stick system, but how is it that Tally Stick treasures never show up in Medieval films, and we don't hear about tally stick frauds or tally stick robberies?

Perhaps the fact that in 1694 the Bank of England at it's formation attacked the Tally Stick System gives us a clue as to why most of us have never heard of it. They realised this was money outside the power of the money changers, (the very thing King Henry had intended).

What better way to eliminate the vital faith people had in this rival currency than to pretend it simply never existed and not discuss it. That seems to be what happened when the first shareholder's in the Bank of England bought their original shares with notched pieces of wood and retired the system. You heard correctly, they bought shares. The Bank of England is a privately owned bank which was actually set up by investors buying shares.

These investors, whose names were kept secret, were meant to invest one and a quarter million pounds, but only three quarters of a million was received when it was chartered in 1694.

It then began to lend out many times more than it had in reserve, collecting interest on the lot.

This is not something you could just impose on people without preparation. The money changers needed to create the climate to make the formation of this private concern seem acceptable.

Here's how they did it.

With King Henry VIII relaxing the Usury Laws in the 1500's, the money changers flooded the market with their gold and silver coins becoming richer by the minute.

The English Revolution of 1642 was financed by the money changers backing Oliver Cromwell's successful attempt to purge the parliament and kill King Charles. What followed was 50 years of costly wars. Costly to those fighting them and profitable to those financing them. The Money Changers.

So profitable that it allowed the money changers to take over a square mile of property still known as the City of London, which remains one of the three main financial centres in the world today.

The 50 years of war left England in financial ruin. The government officials went begging for loans from guess who, and the proposed deal resulted in a government sanctioned, privately owned bank **which could produce money from nothing,** essentially legally counterfeiting a national currency for private gain.

This privately owned bank was and is still known as The Bank of England.

Now the politicians had a source from which to borrow all the money they wanted to borrow, and the debt created was secured against public taxes.

You would think some nations would have seen through this, and realised they could produce their own money and owe no interest, but instead the Bank of England has been used as a model and now nearly every nation has a Central Bank which is privately controlled.

These central banks have the power to take over a nation's economy and become that nation's real governing force. What we have here is a scam of mammoth proportions covering what is actually a hidden tax, being collected by private concerns.

The country sells bonds to the bank in return for money it cannot raise in taxes. The bonds are paid for by money produced from thin air. The government pays interest on the money it borrowed by borrowing more money in the same way. There is no way this debt can ever be paid, it has and will continue to increase.

If the government did find a way to pay off the debt, the result would be that there would be no bonds to back the currency, so to pay the debt would be to kill the currency.

Meanwhile it's the money changers who keep getting richer.

With it's formation the Bank of England soon flooded Britain with money. With no quality control and no insistence on value for money, prices doubled with money being thrown in every direction.

One company was even offering to drain the Red Sea to find Egyptian gold lost when the sea closed in on the pursuers of Moses.

By 1698 the national debt expanded from £1,250,000 to £16,000,000 and up went the taxes the debt was secured on.

While the central bank expresses it's determination to prevent the ups and downs of booms and depressions, there have been nothing but ups and downs since its formation, and the British pound has rarely been stable.

One thing however has been stable and that is the growing fortune of:

THE ROTHSCHILDS (1743)

A goldsmith named Amshall Moses Bower opened a counting house in Frankfurt Germany in 1743. He placed a Roman eagle on a red shield over the door prompting people to call his shop the Red Shield Firm pronounced in German "Rothschild".

His son later changed his name to Rothschild when he inherited the business. Loaning money to individuals was all well and good but he soon found it much more profitable loaning money to governments and kings. It always involved much bigger amounts, always secured from public taxes.

Once he got the hang of things, he set his sights on the world by training his five sons in the art of money creation, before sending them out to the major financial centres of the world to create and dominate the central banking systems.

J.P. Morgan was thought by many to be the richest man in the world during the second world war, but upon his death it was discovered he was merely a lieutenant within the Rothschild empire owning only 19% of the J.P. Morgan Companies.

"There is but one power in Europe and that is Rothschild."
19th century French commentator

We will explore a little more about the richest family a little later, after we've had a look at:

THE AMERICAN REVOLUTION (1764 - 1781)

By the mid 1700s Britain was at its height of power, but was also heavily in debt.

Since the creation of the Bank of England, they had suffered four costly wars and the total debt now stood at £140,000,000, which in those days was a lot of money.

In order to make their interest payments to the bank, the British government set about a programme to try to raise revenues from their American colonies, largely through an extensive programme of taxation.

There was a shortage of material for minting coins in the colonies, so they began to print their own paper money, which they called Colonial Script. This provided a very successful means of exchange and also gave the colonies a sense of identity. Colonial Script was money provided to help exchange of goods. It was debt free paper money not backed by gold or silver.

The Bank of England asked Benjamin Franklin how he would account for the new found prosperity in the colonies. Franklin replied.

"That is simple. In the colonies we issue our own money. It is called Colonial Script. We issue it in proper proportion to the demands of trade and industry to make the products pass easily from the producers to the consumers.

*In this manner, creating for ourselves our own paper money, we control its purchasing power, and we have **no interest to pay** to no one."*
Benjamin Franklin

America had learned that the people's confidence in the currency was all they needed, and they could be free of borrowing debts. That would mean being free of the Bank of England.

In Response the world's most powerful independent bank used its influence on the British Parliament to press for the passing of the Currency Act of 1764.

This act made it illegal for the colonies to print their own money, and forced them to pay all future taxes to Britain in silver or gold.

Here is what Franklin said after that.
"In one year, the conditions were so reversed that the era of prosperity ended, and a depression set in, to such an extent that the streets of the Colonies were filled with unemployed."
Benjamin Franklin

"The colonies would gladly have borne the little tax on tea and other matters had it not been that England took away from the colonies their money, which created unemployment and dissatisfaction. The inability of the colonists to get power to issue their own money permanently out of the hands of George III and the international bankers was the PRIME reason for the Revolutionary War."
Benjamin Franklin's autobiography

By the time the war began on 19th April 1775 much of the gold and silver had been taken by British taxation. They were left with no other choice but to print money to finance the war.

What I find interesting here is that Colonial Script was actually working so well, it became a threat to the established gold standard.

The idea of issuing money as Franklin put it *"in proper proportion to the demands of trade and industry""* and not charging any interest, was not causing any problems or inflation, but this was alien to the Bank of England which only issues money for the sake of making a profit for it's shareholder's.

THE BANK OF NORTH AMERICA
(1781-1785)

If you can't beat them, join them, might well have been the argument of arms dealer, Robert Morris when suggested he be allowed to set up a Bank of England style central bank in the USA in 1781.

The $400,000 he proposed to deposit, to allow him to loan out many times that through **fractional reserve banking,** must have looked really attractive to the officials of government, already lining up licking their lips, desperate for money, .

What will the people say if we charter a private bank to issue the country's money?, must have been a question which came up at the meeting. It was quickly answered by suggesting it be called The Bank of North America, to make it sound official.

Already spending the money they would be loaned, no one made a fuss when Robert Morris could not actually raise the deposit, and suggested he might use some gold, which had been loaned to America from France instead.

Once in, he simply used **fractional reserve banking,** and loaned himself and his friends the money to buy up all the remaining shares. He then began to loan out money multiplied by this new amount to eager politicians, who were probably too drunk with this new 'power cash' to notice or care how it was done.

The scam lasted five years until in 1785, with the value of American money dropping like a lead balloon. The bank's charter was not renewed.

The shareholder's walking off with the interest did not go unnoticed by the governor who probably wished he had a different family name.

"The rich will strive to establish their dominion and enslave the rest. They always did. They always will... They will have the same effect here as elsewhere, if we do not, by (the power of) government, keep them in their proper spheres."
Governor Morris

FIRST BANK OF THE UNITED STATES
(1791-1811)

It worked once, it will work again. It's been six years. There are a lot of new hungry politicians. Let's give it a try. And so there it was, in 1791, the First Bank of the United States (BUS). Deceptively named not only to sound official but also to take attention away from the **real** first bank which had been shut down.

The initials however gave a clear indication that Americans were once again being taken for a ride. And true to its British model, the name of the investors was never revealed.

Having gotten away with it a second time, some of them probably wished Amshall Rothschild had picked a different time to make his pronouncement from his private central bank in Frankfurt.

"Let me issue and control a nations money and I care not who writes the laws." *Amshall Rothschild*

Not to worry, no one was listening as the American government borrowed 8.2 million dollars from the bank in the first 5 years and prices rose by 72%. And this time round the money changers had learned their lesson and had guaranteed they had a twenty year charter.

The president, who could see this ever increasing debt, with no chance of ever paying it back, had this to say.

"I wish it were possible to obtain a single amendment to our Constitution - taking from the federal government their power of borrowing."
Thomas Jefferson

While the independent press, who had not been bought off yet, called the scam"a great swindle, a vulture, a viper, and a cobra."

As with the **real** first bank, the government had been the only depositor to put up any real money, with the remainder being raised from loans the investors made to each other, using the magic of **fractional reserve banking.**

When time came for renewal of the charter, the bankers warned something really bad would happen if the bank was not re-chartered. The charter was not renewed.

Five month later Britain had attacked America and started the war of 1812.

Meanwhile a short time earlier, another independent Rothschild business, the Bank of France, was being looked upon with suspicion by none other than:

NAPOLEON (1803 - 1825)

He didn't trust the bank, saying:
"The hand that gives is above the hand that takes. Money has no motherland; financiers are without patriotism and without decency: their sole object is gain."
Napoleon Bonaparte

In 1803, instead of borrowing from the bank, Napoleon sold territory west of the Mississippi to the 3rd President of the United States, Thomas Jefferson, for 3 million dollars in gold; a deal known as the Louisiana Purchase.

Three million dollars richer, Napoleon quickly gathered together an army and set about conquering much of Europe.

Each place he went to, Napoleon found his opposition being financed by the Bank of England, making huge profits as Prussia, Austria and finally Russia all went heavily into debt trying to stop him.

Four years later, with the main French army in Russia, Nathan Rothschild took charge of a bold plan to smuggle a shipment of gold through France to finance an attack by the Duke of Wellington from Spain.

Wellington's attack from the south and other defeats eventually forced Napoleon to abdicate. He was exiled to Elba, an Island off the coast of Italy. However in 1815 he escaped from exile and returned to Paris. The French soldiers sent out to capture him instead rallied around their old leader.

By March of that year Napoleon had equipped an army with the help of borrowed money from the Eubard Banking House of Paris.

For both sides of a war to be loaned money from the same privately owned Central Bank is not unusual. Nothing generates debt like war. A Nation will borrow any amount to win. The loser is kept going to the last straw in a vain hope of winning, which insures the maximum resources are used up by the winning side before victory is obtained; and even more amazing, the loans are usually given **on condition that the victor will pay the debts left by the loser.**

With 74,000 French troops led by Napoleon, sizing up to meet 67,000 British and other European Troops 200 miles NE of Paris on June 18th 1815, it was a difficult one to call. Back in London, the *real* potential winner, Nathan Rothschild, was poised to strike in a bold plan to take control of the British stock market, the bond market, and possibly even the Bank of England.

Nathan, knowing that information is power, stationed his trusted agent Rothworth near the battle field.

As soon as the battle was over Rothworth quickly returned to London, delivering the news to Rothschild 24 hours ahead of Wellington's courier.

A victory by Napoleon would have devastated Britain's financial system. Nathan stationed himself in his usual place next to an ancient pillar in the stock market.

This powerful man was not without observers as he hung his head, and began openly to sell huge numbers of British Government Bonds.

Reading this to mean that Napoleon must have won, everyone started to sell their British Bonds as well.

The bottom fell out of the market until you could hardly give them away. Meanwhile Rothschild began to secretly buy up all the hugely devalued bonds at a fraction of what they were worth a few hours before.

In this way Nathan Rothschild captured more in one afternoon than the combined forces of Napoleon and Wellington had captured in their entire lifetimes.

The 19th century became known as the age of the Rothschilds when it was estimated they controlled half of the world's wealth.

While their wealth continues to increase today, they have managed to blend into the background, giving an impression that their power has waned.

They only apply the Rothschild name to a small fraction of the companies they actually control.

Some authors claim that the Rothschilds had not only taken over the Bank of England but they had also in 1816 backed a new privately owned Central Bank in America called The Second Bank of The United States, causing huge problems to the American president. Interestingly but not surprisingly, the new bank's charter was a carbon copy of the previous banks.

ANDREW JACKSON (1828 - 1836)

When the American congress voted to renew the charter of The Second Bank of The United States, Jackson responded by using his veto to prevent the renewal bill from passing. His response gives us an interesting insight.

"It is not our own citizens only who are to receive the bounty of our government. More than eight millions of the stock of this bank are held by foreigners... is there no danger to our liberty and independence in a bank that in its nature has so little to bind it to our country?...
Controlling our currency, receiving our public moneys, and holding thousands of our citizens in dependence... would be more formidable and dangerous than a military power of the enemy.
If government would confine itself to equal protection, and, as Heaven does its rains, shower its favour alike on the high and the low, the rich and the poor, it would be an unqualified blessing. In the act before me there seems to be a wide and unnecessary departure from these just principles."
Andrew Jackson

In 1832 Jackson ordered the withdrawal of government deposits from the Second bank and instead had them put into safe banks.

The Second Banks head, Nicholas Biddle was quite candid about the power and intention of the bank when he openly threatened to cause a depression if the bank was not re-chartered, we quote.

"Nothing but widespread suffering will produce any effect on Congress... Our only safety is in pursuing a steady course of firm restriction - and I have no doubt that such a course will ultimately lead to restoration of the currency and the re-chartered of the bank."
Nicholas Biddle

By calling in existing loans and refusing to issue new loans he did cause a massive depression, but in 1836 when the charter ran out, the Second Bank ceased to function. When asked what he felt was the greatest achievement of his career Andrew Jackson replied without hesitation "I killed the bank!". However we will see this was not the end of private financial influence passing itself off as official when we look at.

ABRAHAM LINCOLN AND THE CIVIL WAR (1861 - 1865)

With the Central Bank killed off, fractional reserve banking moved like a virus through numerous state chartered banks causing the economic instability this form of banking thrives on.

When people lose their homes someone else wins them for a fraction of their worth. Depression is good news to the lender. War causes more debt and dependency than anything else, so if the money changers could not have their Central Bank with a license to print money, a war it would have to be.

We can see from this quote of the then chancellor of Germany that the slaves issue was not the only cause for the American Civil War.

"The division of the United States into federations of equal force was decided long before the Civil War by the high financial powers of Europe. These bankers were afraid that the US, if they remained as one block, and as one nation, would attain economic and financial independence, which would upset their financial domination over the world."
Otto von Bismark chancellor of Germany

On the 12th of April 1861 this economic war began.

Predictably Lincoln, needing money to finance his war effort, went with his secretary of the treasury to New York to apply for the necessary loans. The money changers wishing the Union to fail offered loans at 24% to 36%. Lincoln declined the offer.

An old friend of Lincoln's, Colonel Dick Taylor of Chicago, was put in charge of solving the problem of how to finance the war.

His solution is recorded as this.

"Just get Congress to pass a bill authorising the printing of full legal tender treasury notes... and pay your soldiers with them and go ahead and win your war with them also."
Colonel Dick Taylor

When Lincoln asked if the people of America would accept the notes Taylor said.

"The people or anyone else will not have any choice in the matter, if you make them full legal tender. They will have the full sanction of the government and be just as good as any money; as Congress is given that express right by the Constitution."
Colonel Dick Taylor

Lincoln agreed to try this solution and printed 450 million dollars worth of the new bills using green ink on the back to distinguish them from other notes.

"The Government should create, issue, and circulate all the currency and credit needed to satisfy the spending power of the Government and the buying power of consumers....

The privilege of creating and issuing money is not only the supreme prerogative of Government, but it is the Government's greatest creative opportunity. By the adoption of these principles... the taxpayers will be saved immense sums of interest. Money will cease to be master and become the servant of humanity."
Abraham Lincoln

From this we see that the solution worked so well Lincoln was seriously considering adopting this emergency measure as a permanent policy.

This would have been great for everyone except the money changers who quickly realised how dangerous this policy would be for them. They wasted no time in expressing their view in the London Times. Oddly enough, while this article seems to have been designed to discourage this creative financial policy, in its criticism we really can see many of the good points.

"If this mischievous financial policy, which has its origin in North America, shall become endurated down to a fixture, then that Government will furnish its own money without cost.
It will pay off debts and be without debt. It will have all the money necessary to carry on its commerce. It will become prosperous without precedent in the history of the world. The brains, and wealth of all countries will go to North America. That country must be destroyed or it will destroy every monarchy on the globe."
Times of London

From this extract you will see that it is **the advantage provided** by the adopting of this policy which poses a threat to those not using it.

1863, nearly there, Lincoln needed just a bit more money to win the war, and seeing him in this vulnerable state, knowing that the president could not get the congressional authority to issue more greenbacks, the money changers proposed the passing of the National Bank Act. The act went through.

From this point on the entire US money supply would be created out of debt by bankers buying US government bonds and issuing them from reserves for bank notes.

The greenbacks continued to be in circulation until 1994, but their numbers were not increased but in fact decreased.

"In numerous years following the war, the Federal Government ran a heavy surplus. It could not (however) pay off its debt, retire its securities, because to do so meant there would be no bonds to back the national bank notes. To pay off the debt was to destroy the money supply."
John Kenneth Galbrath

America's economy has been based on government debt since 1864 and it is locked into this system. Talk of paying off the debt without first reforming the banking system is just talk and a complete impossibility.

That same year Lincoln had a pleasant surprise. Turns out the Tsar of Russia, Alexander II, was well aware of the money changers scam. The Tsar was refusing to allow them to set up a central bank in Russia.

If Lincoln could limit the power of the money changers and win the war, the bankers would not be able to split America and hand it back to Britain and France as planned. The Tsar knew that this handing back would come at a cost which would eventually need to be paid back by attacking Russia, it being clearly in the money changers sights.

The Tsar declared that if France or Britain gave help to the South, Russia would consider this an act of war. Britain and France would instead wait in vain to have the wealth of the colonies returned to them, and while they waited Lincoln, won the civil war.

With an election coming up the next year, Lincoln himself would wait for renewed public support before reversing the National Bank Act he had been pressured into approving during the war.

Lincoln's opposition to the central banks financial control and a proposed return to the gold standard is well documented. He would certainly have killed off the national banks monopoly had he not been killed himself only 41 days after being re-elected.

The money changers were pressing for a gold standard because gold was scarce and easier to have a monopoly over.

Much of the world's supply was already in their hands and each gold merchant was well aware that what he really had could be easily made to seem like much much more.

Silver would only widen the field and lower the share so they pressed for...

THE RETURN OF THE GOLD STANDARD (1866 - 1881)

"Right after the Civil War there was considerable talk about reviving Lincoln's brief experiment with the Constitutional monetary system. Had not the European money-trust intervened, it would have no doubt become an established institution."
W.Cleon Skouse.

Even after Lincoln's death, the idea that America might print its own debt free money set off warning bells throughout the entire European banking community.

On April 12th in 1866, the American congress passed the Contraction Act, allowing the treasury to call in and retire some of Lincoln's greenbacks, With only the banks standing to gain from this, it's not hard to work out the source of this action.

To give the American public the false impression that they would be better off under the gold standard, the money changers used the control they had to cause economic instability and panic the people.

This was fairly easy to do by calling in existing loans and refusing to issue new ones, a tried and proven method of causing depression. They would then spread the word through the media they largely controlled that the lack of a single gold standard was the cause of the hardship which ensued, while all this time using the Contraction Act to lower the amount of money in circulation.

It went from $1.8 billion in circulation in 1866 allowing $50.46 per person,
to $1.3 billion in 1867 allowing $44.00 per person,
to $0.6 billion in 1876 making only $14.60 per person and down
to $0.4 billion only ten years later leaving only $6.67 per person
and a population continually growing.

Most people believe the economists when they tell us that recessions and depressions are part of the natural flow, but in truth the money supply is controlled by a small minority who have always controlled it and will continue to do so if we let them.

By 1872 the American public was beginning to feel the squeeze, so the Bank of England, scheming in the back rooms, sent Ernest Seyd, with loads of money to bribe congress into demonetising silver.

Ernest **drafted the legislation himself,** which came into law with the passing of the Coinage Act, effectively stopping the minting of silver that year. Here's what he said about his trip, obviously pleased with himself.

"I went to America in the winter of 1872-73, authorised to secure, if I could, the passage of a bill demonetising silver. It was in the interest of those I represented - the governors of the Bank of England - to have it done. By 1873, gold coins were the only form of coin money." Ernest Seyd

Within three years, with 30% of the work force unemployed, the American people began to harken back to the days of the greenbacks and silver backed money.

The US Silver Commission was set up to study the problem and responded with telling history:

"The disaster of the Dark Ages was caused by decreasing money and falling prices... Without money, civilisation could not have had a beginning, and with a diminishing supply, it must languish and unless relieved, finally perish. At the Christian era the metallic money of the Roman Empire amounted to $1,800,million. By the end of the fifteenth century it had shrunk to less than $200,million. History records no other such disastrous transition as that from the Roman Empire to the Dark Ages..."
United States Silver Commission

While they obviously could see the problems being caused by the restricted money supply, this declaration did little to help the problem, and in 1877 riots broke out all over the country. The bank's response was to do nothing except to campaign *against* the idea that greenbacks should be reissued.

The American Bankers Association secretary James Buel expressed the bankers attitude well in a letter to fellow members of the association. He wrote:
"It is advisable to do all in your power to sustain such prominent daily and weekly newspapers, especially the Agricultural and Religious Press, as will oppose the greenback issue of paper money and that you will also withhold patronage from all applicants who are not willing to oppose the government issue of money.

To repeal the Act creating bank notes, or to restore to circulation the government issue of money will be to provide the people with money and will therefore seriously affect our individual profits as bankers and lenders. See your congressman at once and engage him to support our interest that we may control legislation."
James Buel American Bankers Association

What this statement exposes is the difference in mentality between the average person and a banker. With a banker ' less really is more' and every need, an opportunity to exploit.

James Garfield became President in 1881 with a firm grasp of where the problem lay.

"Whosoever controls the volume of money in any country is absolute master of all industry and commerce... And when you realise that the entire system is very easily controlled, one way or another, by a few powerful men at the top, you will not have to be told how periods of inflation and depression originate."
James Garfield

Within weeks of releasing this statement President Garfield was assassinated.

The cry from the streets was to...

FREE SILVER (1891 - 1912)

"Fleecing of the flock" is the term the money changers use for the process of booms and depressions which make it possible for them to repossess property at a fraction of it's worth. In 1891 a major fleece was being planned.

"On Sept. 1st, 1894, we will not renew our loans under any consideration. On Sept. 1st we will demand our money. We will foreclose and become mortgagees in possession. We can take two-thirds of the farms west of the Mississippi, and thousands of them east of the Mississippi as well, at our own price... Then the farmers will become tenants as in England..."
1891 American Bankers Association as printed in the Congressional Record of April 29, 1913

The continued gold standard made this possible.

William Jennings Bryan was the Democratic candidate for president in 1896, campaigning to bring silver back as a money standard. (free Silver)

"We will answer their demand for a gold standard by saying to them: You shall not press down upon the brow of labour this crown of thorns, you shall not crucify mankind upon a cross of gold."
William Jennings Bryan

Of course the money changers supported his opposition on the Republican side so long as he wanted the gold standard maintained. The factory bosses were somehow convinced to tell their work force that business would close down if Bryan was elected, and everyone would lose their jobs.

The Republicans won by a small margin.

Bryan tried again in 1900 and in 1908 but lost both times. He became secretary of state under Wilson in 1912 but became disenchanted and resigned in 1915 under suspicious circumstances connected with the sinking of the Lusitania which drove America into the First World War .

J.P.MORGAN AND THE CRASH OF 1907

If you want to work out the cause of the crash of 1907, checking who benefited is where you might like to look first.

With the stock market slump causing most of the over extended banks to falter little by little, J.P. Morgan offers to save the day. People will do strange things when in a panic, and this might explain why Morgan was authorised to print $200 million from nothing, which he then used to prop things up.

Some of the troubled banks with less than 1% in reserve had no choice. It was accept this solution or go under. Even if they had worked out that their problems had been caused by the same people now offering the solution, there is not a lot they could have done about it.

J.P.Morgan was hailed a hero.

"All this trouble could be averted if we appointed a committee of six or seven men like J.P.Morgan to handle the affairs of our country."
Woodrow Wilson

But not everyone was fooled.

"Those not favourable to the money trust could be squeezed out of business and the people frightened into demanding changes in the banking and currency laws which the Money Trust would frame."
Rep. Charkes A. Lindbergh (R-MN)

Causing booms and busts is the tried and proven method of raking in massive wealth, and what people often forget when they lose what they have, is that in the process someone else has won it.

Apart from making a small number rich at the expense of the many, in this case the instability also served the second purpose of encouraging the public to believe that they would be better off living under a Central Bank and a Gold Standard.

Desperate people have little time for logic.

LINCOLN WATCHES

The statue of Lincoln sitting in his chair, which we all recall when we hear his name, sits facing a building called the Federal Reserve Headquarters.

This institution would not be there if Lincoln had lived to finish his second term in office.

It is not Federal and it has doubtful reserves. The name is an open deception designed to give this **private bank** the appearance that it is operating in the public's interest, when in fact it is run solely to gain private profit for its select stock holders.

It came into being as the result of one of the slickest moves in financial history.

On 23rd December 1913 the house of representatives had passed the Federal Reserve Act, but it was still having difficulty getting it out of the senate. Most members of congress had gone home for the holidays, but unfortunately the senate had not adjourned *sine dei* (without day) so they were technically still in session. There were only three members still present. On a unanimous consent voice vote the 1913 Federal Reserve Act was passed. No objection was made, possibly because there was no one there to object.

Charles Lindbergh would have objected.

"The financial system has been turned over to... the federal reserve board. That board administers the finance system by authority of... a purely profiteering group. The system is private, conducted for the sole purpose of obtaining the greatest possible profits from the use of other peoples money."
Rep Charles A, Lindbergh (R-MN)

Louis T. McFadden would have objected.

"We have in this country one of the most corrupt institutions the world has ever known. I refer to the Federal Reserve Board... This evil institution has impoverished... the people of the United States... and has practically bankrupted our Government.
It has done this through... the corrupt practice of the moneyed vultures who control it."
Rep. Louis T, McFadden (R-PA)

Barry Goldwater would also have objected.

"Most Americans have no real understanding of the operation of the international money lenders... <u>The accounts of the Federal Reserve System have never been audited</u>. It operates outside the control of Congress and... manipulates the credit of the United States."
Sen. Barry Goldwater (R-AZ) underline added

Most Americans would object if they knew.

The Federal Reserve is the largest single creditor of the United States Government, and they are also the people who decide how much the average persons car payments are going to be, what their house payments are going to be, and whether they have a job or not.

Along with Thomas Jefferson who said:
"I sincerely believe that banking institutions are more dangerous to our liberties than standing armies. The issuing power should be taken from the banks and restored to the people to whom it properly belongs."
Thomas Jefferson

The three people who passed the Federal Reserve Act in 1913, knew exactly what they were doing when they set up this private bank, modelled on the Bank of England and the fact that THE BANK OF ENG-LAND had been operating independently unopposed since 1694 must have given them a great deal of confidence indeed.

WHERE THERE'S WAR THERE'S MONEY

War uses up more materials more quickly than anything else on earth. In war expensive equipment doesn't wear out slowly, it gets blown up.

So there it was, the newly formed Federal Reserve poised to produce any money the U.S. Government might need from thin air with each dollar standing to make a healthy interest and all that war machinery slowly wearing out in the base camps.

Nine days after it's formation the Federal Reserve founders were wishing each other a Happy New Year. What good fortune might 1914 bring?

(It's interesting to note that during the 119 year period from founding the Bank of England to Napoleon's defeat at Waterloo, England had been at war for 56 years, while the rest of the time preparing for it, and the whole time making huge profits for the money changers.)

WORLD WAR 1 (1914 -18)

The Germans borrowed money from the German Rothschilds bank, the British from the British Rothschilds bank, and the French from the French Rothschilds. American super banker J.P. Morgan was also a sales agent for war materials. Six months into the war his spending of $10 million a day made him the largest consumer on the planet.

The Rockefellers and the head of president Willson's War Industries Board, Bernard Baruch each made some 200 million dollars while families contributed their sons to the bloody front lines, but profit was not the only motive for involvement.

Russia had spoiled the money changers plan to split America in two, and remained the last major country not to have it's own central bank. Now they would pay for their stubborn independence.

Three years after the start of the war the entire Russian Royal Family was killed and Communism began.

You might find it strange to learn that the Russian Revolution was also fuelled with British money. Capitalist businessmen financing Communism?

Author Gary Allen gives his explanation:

"If one understands that socialism is not a share-the-wealth program, but is in reality a method to consolidate and control the wealth, then the seeming paradox of super-rich men promoting socialism becomes no paradox at all. Instead, it becomes logical, even the perfect tool of power-seeking megalomaniacs.

Communism or more accurately, socialism, is not a movement of the downtrodden masses, but of the economic elite."
Gary Allen, Author

As W.Cleon Skousen wrote in his book "The Naked Capitalist".

"Power from any source tends to create an appetite for additional power... It was almost inevitable that the super-rich would one day aspire to control not only their own wealth, but the wealth of the whole world.

To achieve this, they were perfectly willing to feed the ambitions of the power-hungry political conspirators who were committed to the overthrow of all existing governments and the establishments of a central world-wide dictatorship."
W.Ceon Skousen

Extreme revolutionary groups were controlled by being financed when they complied and cut off, with money sometimes being given to their opposition, when they didn't.

If you find this hard to believe, listen to what the so called dictator of the new Soviet Union had to say.
"The state does not function as we desired. The car does not obey. A man is at the wheel and seems to lead it, but the car does not drive in the desired direction. It moves as another force wishes."
Vladimir Lenin

Rep. Louis T. McFadden, chairman of the House Banking and Currency Committee throughout the 1920-30s explained it this way.

"The course of Russian history has, indeed, been greatly affected by the operations of international bankers... The Soviet Government has been given United States Treasury funds by the Federal Reserve Board... acting through the Chase Bank.

England has drawn money from us through the Federal Reserve Banks and has re-lent it at high rates of interest to the Soviet Government... The Dnieperstory Dam was built with funds unlawfully taken from the United States Treasury by the corrupt and dishonest Federal Reserve Board and the Federal Reserve Banks."
Rep. Louis T.McFadden (D-PA)

Even when Communism collapsed in the Soviet Union, Boris Yeltsin revealed that most of the foreign aid was ending up, we quote. *"straight back into the coffers of western banks in debt service."*

WORLD DOMINATION

With Russia down the money changers now had control of every major national economy. Like a steam roller moving and a wolf gathering it's pack, there was only one thing left to do and that was to go global. The first attempt was the proposal at the Paris Peace Conference after WWI to set up the League of Nations. Old habits die hard, and even what they called 'the war to end all wars' was not enough to convince nations to dissolve their boundaries. The League died.

If politicians really were being controlled, you would think at least one would break ranks and cry out against it. Many did. One was no less than the president of the United States speaking before his death in 1919.

"These International bankers and Rockefeller-Standard Oil interests control the majority of newspapers and the columns of these papers to club into submission or drive out of public office officials who refuse to do the bidding of the powerful corrupt cliques which compose the invisible government."
Theodore Roosevelt

Another was the Mayor of New York expanding on Roosevelt's statement in 1922.

"The warning of Theodore Roosevelt has much timeliness today, for the real menace of our republic is this invisible government which like a giant octopus sprawls its slimy length over City, State, and nation... It seizes in its long and powerful tentacles our executive officers, our legislative bodies, our schools, our courts, our newspapers, and every agency created for the public protection...

To depart from mere generalisations, let me say that at the head of this octopus are the Rockefeller-Standard Oil interest and a small group of powerful banking houses generally referred to as the international bankers. The little coterie of powerful international bankers virtually run the United States government for their own selfish purposes.

They practically control both parties, write political platforms, make catspaws of party leaders, use the leading men of private organisations, and resort to every device to place in nomination for high public office only such candidates as will be amenable to the dictates of corrupt big business...

These international bankers and Rockefeller-Standard Oil interests control the majority of newspapers and magazines in this country."
John Hylan, Mayor of New York. 1922

These warnings fell on deaf ears, drowned out by the music and excitement of the roaring 20's. People don't tend to complain much in times of prosperity, so the money changers used this boom time they had created to defuse any complaints about their growing control.

DEPRESSION IN 1929

Stack in front of you the biographies of all the Wall Street giants, J.P. Morgan, Joe F. Kennedy, J.D Rockefeller, Bernard Baruch, and you'll find they all marvel at how they got out of the stock market and put their assets in gold just before the crash.

None mention a secret directive, since revealed, sent by the father of the Federal Reserve, Paul Warburg, warning of the coming collapse and depression.

With control of the press and the education system, few Americans are aware that the Fed caused the depression. It is however a well known fact among leading top economists.

The Federal Reserve definitely caused the Great depression by contracting the amount of currency in circulation by one-third from 1929 to 1933."
Milton Friedman, Nobel Prize winning economist

"It was not accidental. It was a carefully contrived occurrence... The international bankers sought to bring about a condition of despair here so that they might emerge as rulers of us all."
Rep. Louis T.McFadden (D-PA)

"I think it can hardly be disputed that the statesmen and financiers of Europe are ready to take almost any means to re-acquire rapidly the gold stock which Europe lost to America as the result of World War I."
Rep. Louis T.McFadden (D-PA)

If I told you I'd made an elephant disappear, would you believe me without question? Strange no one questioned it when they were told that 40 billion dollars had **vanished** in the crash.

It didn't really vanish, it simply shifted into the hands of the money changers. This is how Joe Kennedy went from having 4 million dollars in 1929 to having over 100 million in 1935.

During this time the Fed caused a 33% reduction of the money supply, causing deeper depression.

HOW THE FED CREATES MONEY

We've been talking about how the privately owned Federal Reserve can produce money from thin air. Here is how it's done.

1. The purchase of bonds is approved by the Federal Open Market Committee.

2. The Fed buys the bonds, which it pays for with electronic credits made to the sellers bank.. These credits are based on nothing.

3. The receiving banks then use these credits as reserves from which they can loan out ten times the amount.

To reduce the amount of money in the economy they simply reverse the process.

The Fed sells bonds to the public and money is drawn from the purchaser's bank to pay for them.

Each million withdrawn lowers the banks ability to loan by 10 million.

The Federal bank in this way has overall control of the US money supply, as each country's central bank does in the same way. The bankers through the magic of **fractional reserve banking** have been delegated the right to create 90% of the money supply.

This control makes a mockery of any elected government. It places your so called leaders behind a toy steering wheel, like the plastic ones we used to find on dash boards, set up to amuse small children.

Or as Rep.Charles Lindbergh, father of famous aviator Lucky Lindy puts it when commenting on the Federal Reserve Act:

"This act establishes the most gigantic trust on earth. When the President signs this bill, the invisible government by the Monetary Power will be legalised.

The people may not know it immediately, but the day of reckoning is only a few years removed... The worst legislative crime of the ages is perpetrated by this banking bill."
Rep. Charles Lindbergh (R-MN)

Or as Woodrow Wilson put it:

We have come to be one of the worst ruled, one of the most completely controlled governments in the civilised world - no longer a government of free opinion, no longer a government by... a vote of the majority, but a government by the opinion and duress of a small group of dominant men.

Some of the biggest men in the United States, in the field of commerce and manufacture, are afraid of something. They know that there is a power somewhere so organised, so subtle, so watchful, so interlocked, so complete, so pervasive, that they had better not speak above their breath when they speak in condemnation of it."
Woodrow Wilson

In order to clearly establish that this is not a conspiracy theory, but is actually how things are controlled, we further quote Charles Lindbergh. From the house of representatives Lindbergh was well placed to see exactly what was happening then, and continues to happen today.

"To cause high prices all the federal reserve board will do will be to lower the re-discount rate..., producing an expansion of credit and a rising stock market; then when... business men are adjusted to these conditions, it can check... prosperity in mid-career by arbitrarily raising the rate of interest.

It can cause the pendulum of a rising and falling market to swing gently back and forth by slight changes in the discount rate, or cause violent fluctuations by greater rate variation, and in either case it will possess inside information as to financial conditions and advance knowledge of the coming change, either up or down.

This is the strangest, most dangerous advantage ever placed in the hands of a special privilege class by any Government that ever existed.

The system is private, conducted for the sole purpose of obtaining the greatest possible profits from the use of other people's money.

They know in advance when to create panics to their advantage. They also know when to stop panic. Inflation and deflation work equally well for them when they control finance..."
Rep. Charles Lindbergh (R-MN)

ADOLF'S BANKERS

Most all will be aware of Hitler's rise to power. What they probably don't know is that he was almost completely financed by money drawn from the privately owned American Federal Reserve.

"After WWI, Germany fell into the hands of the international bankers. Those bankers bought her and they now own her, lock, stock, and barrel. They have purchased her industries, they have mortgages on her soil, they control her production, they control all her public utilities.

The international German bankers have subsidised the present Government of Germany and they have also supplied every dollar of the money Adolph Hitler has used in his lavish campaign to build up threat to the government of Bruening.

When Bruening fails to obey the orders of the German International Bankers, Hitler is brought forth to scare the Germans into submission...

Through the Federal Reserve Board over $30 billion of American money has been pumped into Germany. You have all heard of the spending that has taken place in Germany...

Modernistic dwellings, her great planetariums, her gymnasiums, her swimming pools, her fine public highways, her perfect factories. All this was done on our money. All this was given to Germany through the Federal Reserve Board. The Federal Reserve Board has pumped so many billions of dollars into Germany that they dare not name the total."
Congressman Louis T.McFadden (D-PA) who served twelve years as Chairman of the Committee on Banking and Currency.

FORT KNOX

In 1933 new President Franklin D. Roosevelt signed a bill forcing all the American people, to hand over all their gold at base rate with the exception of rare coins. He disowned the bill claiming not to have read it with his secretary of the treasury claiming this was "what the experts wanted".

Bought at bargain basement price with money produced from nothing by the Federal Reserve, the gold was melted down and stacked in the newly built bullion depository Fort Knox. Once collected in 1935, the price of gold was raised from $20.66 up to $35 per ounce, but only non American gold could be sold. This meant those who had avoided the crash by investing in gold they had shipped to London could now nearly double their money while the rest of America starved.

But that's not all folks. By the end of WWII Fort Knox did hold 70% of the world's gold, but over the years it was sold off to the European money changers while a public audit of Fort Knox reserves was repeatedly denied.

Rumours spread about missing gold.
"Allegations of missing gold from our Fort Knox vaults are being widely discussed in European circles. But what is puzzling is that the Administration is not hastening to demonstrate conclusively that there is no cause for concern over our gold treasure - if indeed it is in a position to do so."
Edith Roosevelt

Finally in 1981 President Ronald Reagan was convinced to have a look into Fort Knox with a view to re-introducing the Gold Standard. He appointed a group called The Gold Commission. They found that the US Treasury owned no gold at all.

All the Fort Knox gold remaining is now being held as collateral by the Federal Reserve against the national debt. Using credits made from nothing, the Fed had robbed the largest treasure of gold on earth.

WORLD WAR II

World War II saw the US debt increased by 598%, while Japan's debt went up by 1,348%, with France up by 583% and Canada up by 417%.

When you hear this, what is your first impression? Do you automatically think this is bad or this is good? Most of us feel a well programmed sense of desperation when we hear figures like this, but remember, to the money changers, this is music to their ears.

With the hot war over, the cold war began, the arms race causing more and more borrowing. Now the money changers could really concentrate on global domination.

Step one, the European Monetary Union and NAFTA.

Step two, centralise the global economy via the World Central Bank and GATT.

THE WORLD CENTRAL BANK (1948 - Present)

In Washington, the headquarters of both the World Bank and the IMF (International Monetary Fund) face each other on the same street. What are these organisations, and who controls them?

To find out we need to look back to just after WWI.

At this point the money changers were attempting to consolidate the central banks under the guise of peacemaking. To stop future wars they put forward the formation of a world central bank named the Bank of International Settlements, a world court called the World Court in the Hague, and a world executive for legislation called the League of Nations.

In his 1966 book entitled Tragedy and Hope, president Clinton's mentor Carroll Quigley writes about this.

"The powers of financial capitalism had [a] far-reaching [plan], nothing less than to create a world system of financial control in private hands able to dominate the political system of each country and the economy of the world as a whole.

This system was to be controlled in a feudalist fashion by the central banks of the world acting in concert, by secret agreements arrived at in frequent meetings and conferences.

The apex of the system was to be the Bank for International Settlements in Basel, Switzerland, a private bank owned and controlled by the world's central banks which were themselves private corporations.

Each central bank... Sought to dominate its government by its ability to control treasury loans, to manipulate foreign exchanges, to influence the level of economic activity in the country, and to influence cooperative politicians by subsequent economic rewards in the business world."
Carroll Quigley, Professor, Georgetown University

They got 2 out of 3. The league of nations failed largely owing to the suspicions of the people, and while opposition concentrated on this, the other two proposals snuck their way through.

It would take another war to wear the public resistance down. Wall street invested heavily to rebuild Germany, as the Chase bank had propped up the Russian revolution.

Now the Chase merged with the Warburg's Manhattan Bank to form the ChaseManhattan which would later merge with the Chemical Bank to become the largest bank on Wall Street.

In 1944 the US approved it's full participation in the IMF and the World Bank. By 1945 the second League of Nations was approved under the new name ' **The United Nations** '. The war had dissolved all opposition.

The methods used in the National Banking Act of 1864 and the Federal Reserve Act of 1913 were now simply used on a Global scale.

The Federal Reserve Act allowing the creation of Federal Reserve notes is mirrored by the IMF's authority to produce money called Special Drawing Rights (SDRs). It is estimated the IMF has produced $30 billion dollars worth of SDR's so far. In the United States SDR's are already accepted as legal money, and all other member nations are being pressured to follow suit. With SDR's being partially backed by gold, a world gold standard is sneaking it's way in through the back door, which comes with no objection from the money changers who now hold two-thirds of the worlds gold and can use this to structure the worlds economy to their further advantage.

We have gone from the goldsmith's fraud being reproduced on a national scale through the Bank of England and the Federal Reserve, to a Global level with the IMF and the World Bank. Unless we together stop giving these exchange units their power by our collective faith in them, the future will probably see the Intergalactic Bank and the Federation of Planets Reserve set up in much the same way.

This radical transfer of power has taken place with absolutely no mandate from the people.

Nations borrow Special Drawing Right from the International Monetary Fund in order to pay interest on their mounting debts. With these SDRs produced at no cost, the IMF charges more interest. This, contrary to bold claims, does not alleviate poverty or further any development. It just creates a steady flow of wealth from borrowing nations to the money changers who now control the IMF and the World Bank.

The permanent debt of Third World Countries is constantly being increased to provide temporary relief from the poverty being caused by previous borrowing.

These repayments already exceed the amount of new loans. By 1992 Africa's debt had reached $290 billion dollars, which is two and a half times greater than it was in 1980. A noble attempt to repay it has caused increased infant mortality and unemployment, plus deteriorating schools and general health and welfare problems.

World resources continue to be sucked into this insatiable black hole of greed: if it is allowed to continue the entire world will face a simular fate.

As one Prominent Brazilian Politician put it.

"The Third World War has already started. It is a silent war. Not, for that reason, any less sinister. The war is tearing down Brazil, Latin America, and practically all the Third World. Instead of soldiers dying, there are children. It is a war over the Third World debt, one which has as its main weapon, interest, a weapon more deadly than the atom bomb, more shattering than a laser beam."

If a group or organisation had used its hard earned money to help these developing nations, then we might sympathise that there should be a real effort to repay these loans. But the money used was created from *fractional reserve banking.* The money loaned to the Third World came from the 90% the banks allow themselves to loan on the 10% they actually held. It didn't exist, it was created from nothing, and now people are suffering and dying in an effort to pay it back.

This has gone beyond clever financing, it's wholesale murder and it's time we stopped it. We can!

Please read on to see how....

Part Two

XAT

The Model for a
Tax Free Economy
(the future)

INTEREST FREE Green XAT

"Growing numbers of social and environmental activists and their supporters and sympathisers now recognise that economics as conventionally understood is not an objective science which must be accepted on its own terms, but an unsound way of thinking that mystifies and distorts both the reality and the morality of people's behaviour towards one another and the natural world. They have learned by experience that economic orthodoxy of whatever variety-capitalist, socialist or a mixture of the two-damages what they care about and systematically obstructs what they are trying to do."
James Robertson, from his excellent book Future Wealth, A New Economics for the 21st Century.

The rewards set up by our current economic system encourage resources to be converted into money as soon as possible. Save money and you will get paid interest; save some trees and you get nothing. Take the money you get from selling your trees, invest it at 10%, and with compound interest your money will double in about 9 years. Leave the trees to be harvested in 10 years and you'll make much less. It's definitely more profitable to be less ecologically sound. It's better business to use up resources as quickly as you can so that you can get paid sooner.

An attitude assuming endless supply encourages ever growing expansion, and if you can make more money by drilling up oil or cutting down rain forest today , you will harvest the resources long before they are needed, with no thought for the future effects of this action. While the land you had may not be of any use anymore, you can move somewhere else with the money you earned destroying it. Paying interest is something we accept as normal. The effects on our environment of paying interest really should be questioned.

"Only after the last tree has been cut down, only after the last river has been poisoned, only after the last fish has been caught, only then will you find that money cannot be eaten." is a Cree Indian Prophecy which expresses a great deal of wisdom.

The investment of money has become very impersonal, with many individuals having no idea what atrocities their investments might be supporting.

While a pension fund just represents cash with concern for the interest we can make, most have no concern for the method used to acquire it. Control is handed over to make a profit, and when the results of investments appear on the news as a horror story, we look on with sadness having no idea we helped to cause this. Third world countries lacking proper food and water give most of what they earn to pay back interest on investments made with money made available by people who invested blindly to increase their nest egg. Are you one of them? We have seen that each pound or dollar in your savings account allows ten times that amount to be invested with no restriction, yet most never feel responsible for any damage these investments they make might cause.

Today there are thousands of institutions set up for the exchange and transfer of financial claims, and these are all set up to make money from money. The people and organisations concerned are not interested in efficiency or fairness, but primarily in making a profit for themselves at other peoples expense. The financial system that exists today is systematically corrupt.

While making money out of money accounts for about 95% of all the worlds foreign exchange transactions, only 5% is concerned with the actual trade of goods. The number of those involved in these productless transactions continue to grow and grow.

Imagine someone who buys a few shares in the company which employs them. The shares go up in value so they buy a few more. This pattern is repeated until the shares are earning more than they earn working, so they quit working and live off their share earnings. Seeing this, other workers in the company start to buy shares as well, and soon they are also able to live from their share profits. The word spreads and soon people from nearby villages are joining in. The shares in this company are now in high demand and as a result their value continues to rise and rise. Because of this increase, there is money to be made not only in having shares, but in trading and selling them as well and the number of people living from share related profits soon far exceeds the number the company employs. The people trading shares soon become more important than the people producing the products, and the company's workers are all saving to join them. Trade would probably continue with no one noticing that the company building was empty.

The values held within our present system are not just unfair, they are in fact ridiculous. A new economic order is not only desirable but desperately needed. An overall view of cause and effect needs to be considered to give value to actions which affect us all, considering real people and the Earth's real needs.

A new framework must be both enabling and conserving. Real value of action has to focus on the end result over any short term gain. We must consider how much water will be let in before we burn the hull of the ship to keep warm.

Conventional economics has no regard for sustaining resources or for it's effect on people and the environment. Because we place value on how much money a person earns, we devalue all the other good things people might do for themselves and each other.

What we have today creates an ever decreasing circle designed to allow the rich to get richer. The richer you get the less you have to do, as your money makes more and more money in interest for you, and as that pile of cash grows higher and higher nothing real is produced. Stop everything else and the rich will keep getting richer at the expense of the poor.

SLAVE TO MONEY

Having looked at how our present system came into being, and seeing how a select few have managed to manipulate the whole thing to their advantage, it's time to have a look at the philosophies and beliefs which have made this takeover possible.

While most of us would rather not have a world being held to ransom by national debts, it's strange to realise that none of this could have happened without our combined consent and co-operation.

Since no sane person would vote themselves into slavery, we can only conclude that we have been victims of a con, coercing us into giving this unfair system our support. We will now see how this has happened and how it was made to seem normal.

Any system which has been around for a long time will have developed within it various means to protect itself from being replaced.

An obviously effective form of protection is to give the impression that no other system is possible. People who believe this to be true will never bother to try and find a better way.

By allowing people to vote in deciding different aspects of the system they find themselves under, an illusion can be created which gives individuals the impression that they are somehow in control, but since all the choices given are limited to being within the system which provides them, no real choice can ever be made outside its limits.

This illusion of freedom however comes at a slight risk, but none of the people in charge take that risk seriously. That slight risk is of course that something might be presented to vote for which is not a part of the present system, but in fact better, redistributing the wealth and power in a fairer way.

Much has been done in the cultivation of general attitude to discredit any such suggestion in advance . As a result anyone daring to point the way to something different has their work cut out for them. (No need to pass the scissors.)

THE END OF THE WORLD

In a world full of marvellous inventions which most of us use, but few of us really understand, it's a wonder that new ideas have such a difficult time being taken seriously.

Surrounded by constant development it does seem odd that change is resisted on every corner. Strange until we remember that our present system has probably built this attitude into us for it's survival.

After all, if we considered seriously that there might be a better way, we might try it, and that could be the end of the world **as we now know it.**

Because most of us have been taught to resist change, we continue with things as they are, hoping the next lot of politicians that we vote for might have the answer to our problems.

At the end of the day no matter who you vote for in our present system, you still end up with a politician, who has to toe the party line, and who has very little individual power to change anything.

POWER TO THE PEOPLE

Our common agreement in the value of money is really what makes everything connected with it possible, but this idea is so ingrained, we hardly ever question if our trust might be misplaced.

The word on the streets is often at odds with the attitudes of the governing bodies. For years before the fall of the Berlin wall, most of the people living under communist rule realised things were not right, but most felt powerless to do anything about it. While the rulers were totally dependant upon the people's co-operation, the people were not organised enough to withdraw their support. It was much the same thing in South Africa with apartheid. It takes individuals to realise injustice before a more positive path can be taken by the masses. It is a huge step to go from blindly accepting to quietly questioning. These questions can be the seeds to real positive change and should not be underestimated.

We've seen in our brief look at history that interest free money can indeed provide prosperity, as with Lincoln's Greenbacks and the Colonial Script. Once the people accepted these as legal tender, their real value was never in question, and the fact that the source of cash was not a central bank didn't stop anyone from spending that money or working to earn it. The only losers with Lincoln's greenbacks were those who would have gained from charging interest.

Interest free money is just one step away from tax free money. The significance of Lincoln's clever plan is not much discussed, and the very idea of a Tax Free Economy goes against the current popular logic taught to us in school. Because having taxes collected from us is something which we have grown up with, been told is necessary and can't be avoided, it's hard for us to imagine it being any other way.

As in Russia, the most important and vital force concerned, (people power), remains underestimated and is hardly ever given any credit. Those at the top of the financial tree, who rely totally on those below for their position, take our co-operation for granted. They grin with confidence even during an election, confident in the knowledge that whoever we might vote for we will end up with the same system with them being obscenely rich at the top. The ship we sail on maintains the same course while we are allowed to decide what games get played on deck.

The election process as it is now does not threaten the financial powers that really control things.

While they can see the value in giving us a choice on minor matters, there is no way they are silly enough to risk their privileged position to the will of the people. The real rulers act beyond democracy and with no mandate from us, and they will continue to do so as long as we collectively let them.

TAX COLLECTORS LOVE TAX COLLECTING

Obviously those who rely on tax collection for their living don't encourage people to see it any differently either, yet there have been whole societies which have prospered in the past with no need to collect taxes from anyone.

The whole of North and South America, was once a thriving Tax Free haven, before the settlers arrived and brought with them their dominator ideas.

COMPLICATED ECONOMICS

Economics is something that affects everyone, but only a select few really fully understand.

Even the so called experts on the subject disagree among themselves.

As with a weather person on the telly, an impression can be given of real predictability, but the illusion is easily shattered by a freak storm or a stock market crash, which seems to arrive with little or no warning.

If politicians really did understand how the economy worked, surely with the power they have, they could insure that it constantly ran smoothly.

The fact that it never runs smoothly clearly demonstrates just how little these people really know and how little control they really have.

Those who are capable of manipulating the system are hardly going to brag about it.

As we have seen they thrive on things not running smoothly, but their hidden agenda will never make the news.

If we all realised we were being conned, the con would be over.

The present system relies a great deal on peoples ignorance of it, (as we have seen). Any fair alternative would need to be simple enough for everyone concerned to understand.

A NECESSARY UPGRADE FOR A FAIRER PLAN

To give you a modern day example; computers today are often upgraded by simply adding on a specially produced programme like a new operating system. The basic computer remains the same, but with it's new addition it is able to do things it could not do before.

In the same way a fairer plan can be designed to upgrade our present system, converting but not destroying the useful framework which is already in place.

Whereas the present system is imposed upon us from an outside source, run from back rooms, not allowing our involvement in its day to day direction, any fair plan should rely on our participation and co-operation to work.

Once in place, this new plan should need no politicians to direct it, and no money changers to fleece it, as the ideas and needs of each individual, should rightly be the guiding force. This book suggests a plan for your consideration which fits those guidelines.

All of the technology to accomplish this plan is already in place and no further inventions or interventions are needed to make it work. We already have a fully working model which you will be invited to try and help to improve on.

WHY?

Our present leaders want us to believe that the central banking system is sound and collecting taxes is necessary. Why?

Originally the purpose of collecting taxes was solely to make the collectors and the money changers rich, ie the King or the Queen, and their treasury, but these days taxes are collected supposedly to provide each community with needed services, **(while continuing to make the collectors and money changers as rich as before).** The present system forces people to chip in for the common good, (and it's leader's luxury), while threatening prison for those who refuse to pay.

The aim of providing hospitals, fire engines, rubbish collection, etc. is a good one, but history shows us that borrowing from central banks, and taxing people, are not the only methods available to us to raise this much needed cash.

THE VALUE OF MONEY

Who is entrusted with giving money its value?

The answer may surprise you. The Tally Stick System of King Henry the First will have given us a clue to who is entrusted with this awesome power. (It wasn't the King.)

A five pound note or a dollar bill is a piece of paper with fancy printing on it. Its actual worth, printed in huge quantities as it is, is a fraction of a fraction of a penny.

To produce a simular coupon with similar markings, (watermark and metal strip safe guard), would not cost anyone very much per unit, if they were producing millions of them.

So why are you willing to accept this fancy paper in return for your labour or things you value? Why is a shopkeeper willing to accept this fancy paper in exchange for food or other goods?

This fancy paper is not accepted for goods simply because it is produced by an official mint. It is not accepted because it features fine art work and intricate engraved designs. It's acceptance has nothing to do with whose face is printed on it. That person pictured does not give the cash its value.

There is only one reason why this fancy paper is accepted in exchange for goods or services, and that is because the person accepting it, believes that others will accept this same fancy paper from them in exchange for goods or services, they may wish to purchase in the future.

We believe this fancy paper is worth more than ordinary paper and it is this one belief which gives this paper its worth. We believe that others will share our belief in its worth, and that we will be able to buy things we need or want in the future, so we are willing to part with valuable goods today in exchange for fancy paper we are convinced we can spend tomorrow.

It is we together by our common agreement and belief who give money its value.

The cash exchange system is a fine example of collective faith and the power of mass imagination. If it did not already exist, it would require a massive leap of faith to start up such a thing from scratch.

It would be an extremely difficult thing to introduce out of the blue. Finding that first person willing to accept a bit of paper in return for their labour would be near on an impossible task.

To convince the whole population that previously worthless fancy paper could be transformed into valuable currency, simply by mass agreement, would definitely not be easy.

Fortunately for us, we already have inherited a working example of collective faith in action, which we all demonstrate, each time we exchange these tokens for real goods or services.

If after considering this example, you still doubt that we have the power to make real and valuable anything we agree on, then you might find it useful to consider credit cards, cheques, mortgage deeds, log books and any other forms of contract which involves the exchange of goods.

The plastic, the cheque or the deed paper is not worth very much in itself, but **the agreement it represents** makes it worth what it is believed to be worth.

The real foundation of any agreement is not the words or currency it is written in, but the belief that what is agreed will be delivered.

Hence a piece of plastic can buy you a washing machine, and just the sight of this plastic is enough to convince the shop keeper to have it delivered to your door. The shop keeper is not hypnotised by the hologram on the card to send you the washer, he or she is convinced by the agreement between you, him and the credit card company, that a fair exchange will be received for the product.

Not a lot of emphasis is placed on the need for people to trust in the value of our common agreement because we have reached a stage where we naturally believe in the value of certain tokens without question.

It is none the less true to say that without our common trust in the exchange agreement, trading in money could not take place.

In simpler terms, **if people in general did not believe in the value of money, money would have no real value of itself.**

This easy to see fact, when it's pointed out, is not one which the present system feels the need to explain, but it is vital for us to understand in the unfolding of a fairer economic plan.

GREEN MONEY

Many will already be familiar with the many 'LETS' or green money schemes which exist throughout the world. The XAT plan is more than just a LETS scheme but understanding how these work will be helpful to us.

For those who haven't heard about these, let me briefly explain that these are a method of exchange which require no actual money. This system also relies on a vital general agreement among those who participate to work.

Usually people pay a one time fee to join and are issued with a 'LETS' cheque book, which means they can pay for goods or services from other members using a 'LETS' cheque, or have their account credited by 'LETS' if they provide goods or services to a member. As with a credit card transactions, each deal is entered into a computer to keep track of the accounts.

All of the people involved can advertise their goods and services freely in a directory produced from initial joining fees. It is regularly updated, and made available to the growing number of members from time to time. That briefly is the general idea.

Services can be anything from dog walking to highly skilled work and are usually charged at the going rate, allowing one 'LET' to equal the value of one pound, (or the local exchange unit).

Present 'LETS' schemes usually start each account at 0 and allow participants to build up their balance, some providing credit.

The advantage of being part of such a scheme is that the provider of services or goods will attract extra business from people with 'LETS' in their accounts who might not be able to afford cash, and they will also be able to purchase services from members without needing to spend cash.

Transactions can be made using part 'LETS' and part cash if the parties agree, but the 'LETS' operators do not concern themselves with the cash part of the deal.

While this is a good example of how people agreeing can create a new and valuable form of exchange, the 'LETS' system can only work successfully hand in hand with the present system and is not equipped to replace it. The 'LETS' system does give a boost to the local economy by providing a novel and fresh source of revenue and trade, but if everyone adopted this system fully there would be no revenue for local services to operate on and that would definitely not be a step forward.

The new plan we are unfolding here has all the advantages of the 'LETS' system and requires a similar method to maintain it, but it also has the option for providing **tax free** community services and interest free money.

WHY SO COMPLICATED?

We have noted that the present system seems to be designed to be complicated. One might well ask what advantage there could be to anyone for such a design?

While the methods used are indeed complicated, the reason for using them, is rather simple.

Keeping certain things like the economy in the realm of so called experts places everyone else at the mercy of the designs these experts make.

Take the tampering with interest rates by the central banks or government for instance. Everyone knows it goes on, as they announce it on the news, but most people do not understand the reasoning behind it. Not only would I question the reasoning, but I would also question the morality of doing such a thing as well.

When people are unable to make payments on their homes, land or businesses, these properties are taken by the money lenders/mortgage providers by default. Only individuals lose out, their is no way a bank could ever lose out in this way. We have seen by looking at history, that in times of economic boom and bust, the repossession of property is referred to by experts as the fleecing of the flock. These so called experts understand that money is in and of itself worthless, but they use it's perceived worth in order to get their hands on the various commodities that money represents. Altering interest rates is simply another method of legally stealing from the people.

This sort of action would not be tolerated in any other part of society as being honest, and anyone attempting such a move would be charged and found guilty of fraud. Let me explain.

Say you come to me to buy a table I've advertised in a free paper. The price I want is £500.

You say you can't afford to pay me all at once, so I agree to let you pay in 11 weekly installments of £50 each, making the total £550 from which I will earn £50 extra, to compensate for the time I'll need to wait.

That £50 is my interest, which we both agree is fair.

Four weeks later I come to you, (after you have faithfully made four payments), and I tell you I've decided to raise the price to £600, doubling my interest to £100. I explain nonchalantly I've raised the interest rate.

What might be your reaction to that? Would you just accept the new price or might you call me a few choice names instead, with no fear of being charged with libel?

If an individual tried to pull a stunt like this we would say they are being dishonest, pulling a fast one and not keeping to their word, but when the government or central bank does exactly the same thing, it is accepted without question. The very fact that people lose their property in the process, is simply seen as being one of those things which happens, and no one is ever accused of doing anything underhanded.

To agree one price and then to cause the price to rise before people have had a chance to pay the agreed rate is clearly not an honest practice; but so long as economics is kept a mystery to the average person, this sort of dishonest action is allowed to continue, with no need to explain why to the families who have lost their homes in the process.

Put simply, the more complicated it seems, the more those running things can get away with, without ever needing to justify themselves or their actions.

FAT CATS AND FUNNY IDEAS

It's odd that most people who admit they know nothing about economics still tend to have some very strong views on the subject. This is probably because it's the money changers who own most of the media and determine what is taught in our schools.

Some of these commonly held misconceptions can easily be demonstrated to be incorrect or at best incomplete, but to challenge them would be of no benefit to the present status quo, so people are allowed to keep their misconceptions without question, (until now, that is).

One topic on which people hold strong views is inflation.

Inflation put simply, is like the man in the restaurant who asked for a little bread to finish his soup and a little soup to finish his bread. As the story goes, he is still sitting in that same restaurant to this day, no nearer to finishing his meal than when he started.

So prices go up to match rising wages and wages go up to match rising prices, or is it the other way round? No one really knows.

All we do know for sure is that this process causes a constant rise in prices and wages which goes back as far as anyone can remember, and the result is that the price of a small holding with garden at the turn of the last century will now buy you a set of trainers and a can of cola, (if you hurry).

Meanwhile the time taken to earn an actual product remains about the same.

That is to say for example, in the early 1970's when £30 per week was considered a reasonable wage for working in a supermarket, that £30 would get you your rent, let you do your shopping and leave you enough for some clothes, payments on a major appliance and allow you to go out from time to time. Whereas today you could earn £30 in a day but your weeks wages would not provide any more than your weeks wages 25 years ago.

One thing inflation does do is give people **the impression** that they are earning more for the hours they are working when really that is not the case.

Inflation seems to be a phenomena based on the idea that everyone contributes to it because every one contributes to it. A kind of mass negative agreement.

Most know any gains to be made are really only temporary and likely to be lost as the balance changes, but people continue to play the inflation game because they think everyone else will, and they don't want to be left out.

It's all a bit pointless really but no real problem if a shopkeeper wants to charge 20 times more for a product, so long as the average person is making 20 times as much to pay for it. It does serve to confuse people's perception of value and adds to the general confusion which surrounds economics.

As far as I can see the only way which would successfully encourage people providing products and services to keep their prices stable would be to provide a real incentive for them to do so. With computer information on prices being what it is today, it would be easy to identify producers who continue to provide the same product at the same price over a given amount of time and present them with special grants or bonuses for doing so.

If you issued bonus money to the public which could only be spent in shops which maintain stable prices, many shops would maintain their prices to qualify for this extra business and inflation control would be fun and profitable for all concerned.

Producing interest free money to reward those keeping stable prices is an option we have which could actually help lower inflation.

MAKING MONEY

Oddly enough, if you dare to suggest that we use Lincoln's method to produce a form of greenbacks to meet the country's needs, the politicians argue that this will actually cause inflation. They argue that the more money people have, the more shops will be able to charge for their goods, hence higher prices and new wage demands following quickly to meet them.

Like so many of the system's ideas, this seems quite reasonable when looked at on it's own, but it ceases to make sense when we take a look at the overall picture.

While the government peddles the evils of printing money to meet the country's needs, **it borrows the same money** it needs by producing bonds, which at the end of the day still results in the same money entering the market place.The interest owed will obviously not apply, but interest owed doesn't affect the amount of money in circulation in any case as 'being owed' implies it's not been paid yet.

As we have seen, history demonstrates that bypassing the central banks and producing interest free money **according to need** does not cause any problems. It's not the source of needed money which causes inflation, it's the attitude people have to money in general.

Here is another example as described by David Weston of a scheme in Austria, in the 1930s.

"The burghermaster of Worgl issued local currency in the form of "tickets for services rendered". They were used for paying wages to men employed on public works, who would otherwise have been unemployed. During the first month of issue these tickets are said to have circulated twenty times as a form of local currency. Taxes were paid, unemployment was reduced, and local shopkeepers prospered. Mayors of two hundred other Austrian towns decided to follow suit. But the Austrian National Bank took legal action against the experiment, the Austrian Supreme Court decided in favour of the Bank, and the innovation was squashed."
David Weston, The Living Economy

You might be reading this with the aid of an electric light.

The inventor of that light bulb Thomas Edison also had a keen understanding of politics. Here is what he had to say on the subject:

"If our nation can issue a dollar bond, it can issue a dollar bill. The element that makes the bond good, makes the bill good, also. The difference between the bond and the bill is the bond lets money brokers collect twice the amount of the bond and an additional 20%, where as the currency pays nobody but those who contribute directly in some useful way.

It is absurd to say that our country can issue $30 million in bonds and not $30 million in currency. Both are promises to pay, but one promise fattens the usurers and the other helps the people."
Thomas Edison

Can you tell me from looking at a five pound note if it was borrowed by the government before it reached your pocket? To the end user it makes absolutely no difference where it came from; all that matters is whether you can spend it or not. If Lincoln had not marked his bills with greenbacks as an act of good faith, would anyone have known the difference?

As we have seen, the banking system has always been opposed to governments printing money, and always in favour of governments borrowing money from them instead, but this is not because **responsible production** of money, like the Colonial Script or Greenbacks, doesn't work or causes massive inflation. It's because the money changers can't take their pound of flesh from this sort of money.

Money not backed by gold or silver and money not produced to be loaned at interest is only backed by the people's goodwill, and the central banks can't make any money on goodwill. This is the real reason they are opposed to it.

They have created a complicated logic which they sponsor the teaching of, mainly to hide this one fact. This created logic is perpetuated by those who stand to lose if interest free money is allowed to be produced. This action would put those now supplying the money at interest out of business, and they will do absolutely anything to prevent that from happening.

True, if money is printed with no proper intention and handed out on street corners to people passing by in truck loads, then money will lose it's value, but if money is printed in a controlled way and used to purchase things which the country needs, like the Colonial Scripts and the Greenbacks were produced, according to need, the result will not be any different to that of borrowing the money, except that no interest will be owed on it.

With money to pay for them, the needed services will be provided.

The people providing these social services need have no idea where the money they are being paid with comes from, so nothing different happens. They just go out to the shops and buy things, which contrary to rumour does not upset the shopkeepers one bit. Nor does it inspire them to raise their prices, unless of course they want to see everyone shopping where it's cheaper down the road.

The main and vital difference between handing out money on a street corner and providing money for needed services is that one provides **value for money** while the other does not.

If a reasonable attitude is adopted to the production of money for needs, all the problems connected with such production disappear.

Providing money for real services and products actually contributes to the prosperity of the country in the first place and is naturally controlled by the going rate which things are sold at. So long as no more than the going rate is paid out, there is no unnatural flow of cash within the community.

FIRE ENGINE LOGIC

We can use an example here to illustrate this.

Imagine a community needs a new fire enginc. No one can argue against the usefulness of such a thing. If money is made available to buy it, the community will be one fire engine richer. This will be the end result regardless of where the money comes from to make the purchase.

This action will also have further reaching benefits. The company manufacturing the engine will show a higher profit, those working there will be more secure and all the shops that they frequent will be pleased of their custom.

To meet further orders, more materials will be needed, which is good for those providing them, who will pass on their good fortune as they spend what they have made. Given proper environmental and social concern (which is another topic), communities prosper as the needs of the community are provided for.

But perhaps most important, the fire engine will be there to save lives and property if it is ever needed.

It won't all of a sudden not work because the money that bought it was not borrowed from a central bank. The only thing that won't be working is the central bank's interest plan.

THE MAGIC BIKE

To illustrate again how the creation of money for the community does not have a negative effect, allow me to tell you a mind boggling classic story which may well stem from a real event, and has been told and retold for several generations.

This story is set in a time before cheque guarantee cards, and at a time when it was possible to endorse a cheque and pass it on by signing it on the back.

As the story goes, a well dressed man and his young daughter came into a small town on the little girls birthday and her dad decided to buy her a brand new bike.

The bike cost £50 which was enough to buy a decent product in those days.

The shopkeeper eyeing the man's fine clothes decided to accept a cheque which was to be drawn from a bank in a city nearby. Being very pleased with the 50% profit he had made that day, he proceeded to endorse the cheque, (*sign it on the back*), and went ahead and purchased for himself a new watch .

The Jeweller trusting the bike salesman's judgement accepted the cheque. Having now earned about 50% profit himself on his sale he proceeded to endorse the cheque to buy some new fishing equipment.

And the fishing equipment saleswoman, trusting in the judgement of those before, accepted the cheque which she promptly endorsed to buy that new kitchen table she had been wanting.

This went on to include 10 different merchants who each made roughly 50% profit on each sale and now had goods to represent their good fortune.

Merchant 11, the farmer, decided he wanted the cash to take to an auction, so he went to the city to cash the cheque, only to find the cheque was made of rubber, (ie. it bounced!).

Not being one to despair, he went back and invited all the people who had indorsed the cheque to a meeting at his farmhouse.

As the merchants heard the news and saw the useless cheque being waved in the air, each one felt a sinking feeling as they imagined how they would have to break the news to their families, who were all enjoying so many new things.

But it was Fred the baker who saved the day.

He suggested, instead of everyone having to return all the goods, why not have each of the ten chip in £5. each so the farmer could have his £50 cash and they would all still have a handsome profit for their trouble.

If each did make 50% profit, (which is not unusual), the community ended up about £200 richer.

Our man's little girl got her bike and no one lost a thing!

With the practice of endorsing cheques having been discontinued in our modern day, no one can see this as an invitation to pass bad cheques, but it is an interesting example of how wealth and prosperity can be created from nothing with no loss to anyone concerned.

The interesting thing for us to note here is that all the purchases in this example were made in good faith, except perhaps the first one, and everyone involved from that point on believed the cheque to be worth the £50 it had written on it.

The baker's solution to chip in £5 each was more agreeable than the thought of losing all they had gained, but it was only necessary because the bank lost faith in the cheque's value. Even so, with it's true value finally revealed, all it took was a bit of good faith and no one lost a thing.

That such a thing is possible even in principle seems to defy logic, but it is easier to understand when we remember that it is people's belief which gives a paper token its value, and nothing else. We together have this power to use or misuse.

VALUE FOR MONEY

People who work on market stalls or in shops selling their products will all agree that they would like the folks passing by to have more spending money. The result would be, they hope, more sales for them. The one thing which prevents people from buying things more than anything else is not having the available cash. If people are paid a reasonable wage for providing goods and services, not only does the community benefit first hand, but those who rely on selling products to survive naturally benefit from this new purchasing power.

There is however a principle here which needs to be followed and not strayed from, to provide real benefit with no disadvantage to anyone.

The main point of this principle, which separates it from all the horrors associated with handing out free money on street corners is that we must insist on getting **value for money.**

Remember our ten merchants in our example all got value for money and all had to give value for money, so much so that they were able to contribute £5 each to number 11 (the farmer), and still keep a handsome profit.

As long as value is provided for money, then money will not lose its value, even if it has no value to begin with except the value we give it by agreement.

As soon as the cheque in our example was accepted for the bike, it took on the value of the bike and continued to carry it's value even after it bounced. Remember that number 11 still got his £50 cash.

At one time countries limited themselves to printing only what they could back up with gold or silver which they held. We have seen who really benefits from that method.

While this served as a method of control, it makes about as much sense as deciding only to print a fiver each time a bird flies by.

The amount of metal held in a vault has absolutely no relation to how much food and goods people need to buy. Gold of itself does not have the ability to vary it's quantity according to the needs and growth of the population.

In modern times, with the value of money being agreed, the gold standard has been abandoned. What we have now is currency being valued against other currency.

This is only a step away from valuing currency against the things we purchase to supply community needs, which as a bonus would do away with the need to collect taxes and give us real wealth in useful things for the community.

In other words, if you printed the money you needed to build a hospital, and considered the money you printed to be backed by the hospital you built, you would owe absolutely no interest on it, and you wouldn't need to collect it from anyone.

We might agree that it makes sense to back currency up with something so production of money doesn't get out of control.

In this model the things needed in the community take on this roll **after** the money purchases it and not **before.**

It's a little trick in time.

The end result is a hospital. No taxes to collect, no interest to pay. Now doesn't that sound better than what we have now?

BACKED BY US

We have seen that the very act of accepting the currency's value is all that is needed to give it value. As soon as this newly valuated currency is used to purchase something which the community needs, the newly purchased thing can take over the roll of backing up the money, which was originally backed only by our good faith.

Why should we back this money by our good faith?

I can think of a few good reasons.

By doing so we could provide all our community needs at no interest and save ourselves the expense of paying and collecting taxes.

Plus it would naturally feel good for us to use our power of good faith in such a positive way. Passing that hospital each of us could say "it was my power of good faith that made this happen", and it would remind us that we are all part of something good.

Such an idea does not come without individual contribution, but in this case the contribution needed is your agreement to the currency's value.

In other words you are saying that if the community produces the money it needs to buy a much needed hospital, you agree to accept that money if it is offered to you in return for something you wish to sell, but in actual fact, when that money reaches you, it could look no different to money you may have now, unless we choose to mark it like Lincoln's greenbacks.

Why not? So long as everyone else agrees to do the same, you know you can pass the money on to buy things you might need and have nothing to lose, except your annual tax bill.

At present your good faith is being used to make the money changers richer. Why not use it to help your community instead.

THE GUIDE LINES

If we were to suggest that a policy should be adopted to produce tax free money for community needs, it would be very important for us to make clear the guidelines within which this could be done successfully.

A new policy should be as complete as possible before it is presented for consideration. When you think of tax free money, two concepts should come to mind. They are **"real community needs"** and **"value for money"**.

While interest free money has a good track record, tax free money has yet to be tried.

Tax free money can only work efficiently if it is produced in the proper way and for the right reason. It does have its limits, but its limits are it's strength and its protection.

An unrealistic view is to say if improper use will cause problems, then it's not worth trying. We don't stop using a medicine in correct doses just because an overdose might be fatal. A sensible attitude is to have instructions warning what a safe dose is.

It really is possible to provide needed services to the community interest free without needing to collect taxes. This includes all taxes not just income tax.

If this method is employed simply to provide **real community needs**, then it can work perfectly for an unlimited time. If this method is abused, then it won't work for long. For us to suggest that this method be adopted, it is important that what we are suggesting is clear.

If a community were to attempt to use this method for frivolous things and decoration, or excessive wages to a select few, as is the custom with present government officials who award themselves huge pay rises shortly after being elected, then this plan could easily collapse under such unreasonable demands. So those who now line their pockets by dipping into the community chest will not like this idea one bit, and no doubt they will do their best to try to discredit it using their usual complicated jargon.

While this idea is not much good for people who rely on other people's ignorance for their living, it is excellent for the rest of us who would like to see our communities and our world prosper for the common good.

This is not to say that we should not be allowed frivolous things and decoration, all it means is that this method is not suited to provide non-essential things and the revenue for such things needs to be acquired from different sources such as sponsorship, private contributions or public enterprise.

Common sense needs to be applied to keep this plan within its own creative limits, and if this is clear from the start, the idea of tax free money stands a much better chance of being taken seriously.

To use an example, setting fire to something inside a house can be done safely if that thing is in a fire place, but obviously not if that thing is in the middle of your sitting room carpet. If you mention to someone that you intend to set some wood ablaze in your sitting room, and you neglect to mention that the wood is in fact in your fire place, they might well feel very uncomfortable hearing your suggestion.

So it is here that we need to make really clear what our intention actually is.

To suggest the printing of money, to hand out indiscriminately, could be damaging, and is comparable to lighting that fire on the rug in your front room. But to provide for real community needs, making sure you do get value for money, is like taking care that the fire is safely in the fireplace where it can provide much appreciated warmth to the home.

For the most part common sense will tell us what is necessary and what is not. In the case of a hospital verses a statue, the distinction is very clear. In cases which might seem necessary to some and frivolous to others, we will discuss ways we could resolve such disputes later.

The important point for us here is that no matter where the money is gotten from, we must insist on value for money in order to insure that the money keeps its value. And it is to everyone's advantage that it does.

This concept limits us to making purchases at the going rate and buying things which are really needed to benefit the community as a whole.

That means no champagne dinners for a select few, no chauffeur driven limos and no mansions in the country for those in charge. How sad!

But then again this plan does not need a small group to lord over it while lining their pockets because as we will see, it's general direction can be guided by all those it benefits collectively and in this case that really does mean everyone.

Most people will not mind the plan's limitations when they realise that this means all the necessary things in the community can be provided interest free without needing to tax anyone. Those who object to its limitations are not grasping the idea realistically.

TOO SIMPLE?

There are a lot of you reading this I'm sure who might be wondering, if it's as simple as that, why hasn't it been done already?

Others might point to times in history when certain governments flooded the money market causing people to spend a wheelbarrow full of cash for a loaf of bread. A powerful image.

We cannot avoid addressing these two important questions if we wish to create a new awareness of things which are vital to making this new plan work.

We've learned a lot about where our present taxation system comes from, and what it was originally set up to accomplish. As mentioned briefly before, it was not set up to provide public services, it was set up to make the collectors rich. Being able to claim a share from everyone else's earnings was/is the whole point of being a King or Queen and being able to share in the booty is what social privilege is all about.

But more than just a means of easy revenue, this was and is the **ultimate form of control.**

What greater form of control can you think of than having the whole population working to contribute a share of their earnings to you? And what greater invasion of privacy can you imagine, than having someone routing around in your things looking for your coins?

After all, the present system is just an extension of the dominator systems of the past, and tax collection is the most complete expression of domination there is. Taxation allows those that rule to intrude on the very transactions which each individual needs to make in order to stay alive.

If legislation is the reins of power, taxation is the bit.

It is our contention here, that taxation is unnecessary, but those in power allow it to continue because it is their main source of power and power is not sought by our leaders for them to relinquish it in any way. Power is the prize and their reason for striving to be where they are. It would be going against their own principals to support an economic plan which did not include taxation. This would be for them like going to a restaurant and not eating. Replacing the interest grabbing with fair sharing is a simple idea, but the interest grabber's have been given the power to object and of course they do.

IT'S NEVER BEEN TRIED

But what of the famous examples of inflation spiralling out of control which they are bound to throw at us if we suggest the production of tax free money?

One point I've tried to make more than once due to its importance is that **value for money is vital for money to keep its value.**

Where this rule is not strictly observed money can lose its value, and that is all inflation is, money losing it's value.

There has never been a country so far which has been allowed to redesign its economical model in a way which would demonstrate the viability of the ideas presented here. Each time something even close was tried like Colonial Script and the production of Greenbacks it was stomped on by the central banks before it had a chance to grow.

The interest free money mentioned above, which the Americans produced, did work. It worked so well as to pose a threat to the established banking system.

Those who have read the history section will remember, this money was attacked not because it didn't work, but because it worked **too well,** and robbed the central banks from collecting their interest. It was argued that countries using this method would have an unfair advantage and pose a threat to countries not using it.

And interest free money is just one step away from tax free money, is it not?

This plan having never been tried has never failed and its proper implementation cannot be blamed for ever causing inflation anywhere. Printing money in desperation and paying extortionate prices to try and save a sinking ship, as was the case in Germany before and during the war, (from which the example of the wheelbarrows full of cash for a loaf of bread comes from), does not qualify as a demonstration of the plan we are now unfolding. For one thing, the most important rule, that of getting value for money was not observed in this case.

This **new** no taxation plan needs to be approached in a climate of calm, and not a state of emergency. It needs to be decided upon peacefully as a more desirable alternative, not forced on people in a violent revolution.

AND THE LOSERS ARE?

We have demonstrated that money receives its value from the fact that we all agree it has a value. If we wish to go from there and use this power of agreement to produce a currency to pay for community needs, then we could do so.

So long as a builder knows he can spend the money he is paid, he will be happy to do his part in erecting that new hospital we need. Builders are after all happy to be employed, and their only concern is that the money they receive at the end of the week will be accepted by other people in return for things they need to provide for their families.

It needs no more than that! As long as it can be spent, it makes absolutely no difference where the money has come from. Freshly printed or borrowed from an interest grabbing central bank, it makes no difference at all to it's buying power. As long as we get value for money and pay the going rate, that money will be worth what we pay for and will not lose it's value as it is re-spent.

Apart from the money changers, the only losers in a plan such as this would be those who enjoy having control over others for controls sake (*expressing this through taxation*) and quite frankly people who get their kicks in such a perverted way deserve to lose.

TIME FOR A CHANGE

Children play a game of Monopoly with full concentration until someone wins all the property and money and it's no fun playing anymore.

Most of us realise we are at a stage in history where it's time to start a new game to make things fairer for everyone, but the problem is no one wants to be the first to start on a new path for fear that the rest might not follow. People might say "that's a good idea but it will only work if everyone else agrees to it and I'm not going to be the first to try it". Hence a good idea is abandoned and we continue to live with the disadvantages of our old fashioned ways.

The first step to any change is to suggest it in a reasonable way and answer in advance many of the questions this new idea might pose.

THE INTERNATIONAL VIEW

One such question it is reasonable for us to ask is "What about the international view and how would other countries react if we adopted a tax free money plan?"

Let's imagine the announcement on the news. Other countries would see or be informed that we plan to allow tax free money to be produced to supply community needs, and to consider this money backed by the things it produces instead of raising the same money from central bank borrowing, and/or taxation.

We would assure them that we only intend this method to be used to provide or maintain genuine community needs, and we set ourselves the goal to insure that we get value for the money we produce. Within this very strict control we allow ourselves to print the money we need, and we agree as a community to accept this money as legal tender in exchange for goods or services, because we know everyone else will.

At first the scheme would need to work hand in hand with the present system, much the same as Lincoln's famous greenbacks entered the American money supply alongside the regular American money. That is to say money currently in circulation would remain and not be withdrawn. This means that old versions of our money would still be available if foreign countries preferred that. (Our new money might be marked with a tax free hologram to make the distinction clear.)

You'll remember the interest free Greenbacks were marked with green ink to indicate that they were backed only by American good will, and it was left for other countries to decide whether to accept them or not while former American money was still in circulation. The same would be true here.

We've seen that the Greenbacks continued to be accepted all over the world until 1994 when the US withdrew them from circulation. This unconventional money was accepted without question because other countries, knowing Americans would honour it, knew they had a guaranteed place to spend it. It was money which had definite unquestionable value in the USA regardless of it's unconventional origin.

Knowing that we accept our new currency would give it guaranteed value for purchasing things from us, and if someone wished to trade outside the country, they would have to exchange their money for foreign currency which is what they must do now in any case.

So you see, our recognising of our new currency's value would make it valuable to people from other countries as well. Seeing this system work might encourage other countries to use it too, and we of course would welcome this by honouring *their* new tax free currency, which they no doubt would introduce when they saw how well our no tax interest free plan works. After all, they have central banks which I'm sure they would be pleased to be free from as well.

TIME TO GROW

Let's be realistic. Our present governments are far too set in their ways to introduce a tax free money plan tomorrow, no matter how well it's presented. For such a radical idea to be considered seriously, it needs to be demonstrated and shown to have public support.

A demonstration like this will not be setup overnight. Like a tree it will have to start with a good seed and be given the time to take root and spread it's branches.

If a growing number of people began to see the advantages of accepting a new tax free currency, then their example would encourage others to join in. In this way we wouldn't need to make any sudden changes and we could gently flow from the old system to our new plan with no risk of upsetting anything. The old method would be fazed out like the mechanical typewriter and replaced by an easier more efficient and fairer plan. There would be no need for uprising or demonstration. The old method could just simply be respectfully retired.

Remember we are only suggesting building onto what we already have, and upgrading what we already know.

For a while the two methods of trade should work hand in hand, until we are confident enough to switch over completely and eliminate the need to collect taxes altogether.

THE BASIC START

To start off with, an accounts network, no more complicated than what credit card companies now use, needs to be set up to allow transactions to take place in a new freer currency.

That is the most complicated part as it needs a very basic philosophy for common good that won't offend anyone, and a special computer programme designed specifically for it's needs. It would also need to be easily accessible.

Using proceeds from this book, such a computer network already exists.

You don't even need to be on the internet to use it, as it allows transactions to be made from any touch tone phone. Already fully operational, it can be upgraded in stages as more and more people join in.

It's important to mention here that this plan is non-profit making and self financing, with built in promotion. It is designed to be owned by everyone who takes part, and allows everyone to have a say in its future development.

Complete with a security PIN system, this high tech computer based service came on line on the 18th of December 1999. It is very easy to use, as it talks you through each stage of the transaction, and all the accounting is automatic, providing you with your account balance instantly after each transaction.

The system is designed to only respond to phone dial tones, so it is completely isolated from access by computer hackers.

Each transaction is separately recorded and backed up regularly.

HOW IT WORKS

Anyone joining the plan at any stage benefits from being able to make transactions in XAT units with other members and is making a real statement for fairer trade. We realised that in the early stages there would not be a huge number of people to trade with, so to encourage people to take part early on, we created a unique bonus incentive **which increases for early joiners** with each new edition we release, up to and **stopping at edition 21**.

We figure by edition 21 there should be enough people involved to encourage others to join without needing a bonus. It's important to add at this point that you don't have to join the bonus system to take part in XAT trading. Anyone can have a regular account set up, and for this basic service no fee is required. You will be given 100 units to start you off, and if at a later date you want to upgrade to a bonus account you can, (see the form on our web site **www.xat.org).**

Either you spotted this in a shop, on the net, or chances are you have received the copy you are reading free through the post. **If it just arrived, this did not happen by accident.** A friend of yours has paid for, and arranged for us to send this copy of XAT directly to you.

Why have they selected you?

We could say it's because they believe you are a person with foresight and imagination, but it might also have to do with the fact that **sending copies of this to two friends is the only way to qualify for a free bonus account connection to the X.A.T. trading network.**

If you received this in the post, your friend who paid for it has received their new trading account number and their access PIN, which means they can now trade with other members.

They also can look forward to receiving directories of services and products, plus regularly updated information on web site directories and news on the growth of this plan.

But perhaps even more impressive than that, **they have made themselves eligible for the bonus we mentioned.** Here are the details of how the bonus plan works.

THE EARLY BIRD GETS THE BONUS

To qualify for a bonus account you need to order two paperback copies of XAT for two of your friends which will cost you a total of seven pounds sterling including postage and packing.

There is nothing else for you to pay.

On the day you order your 2 copies **we will fill the order with whatever version we have in print at the time. With <u>each new edition</u> we issue after that, the computer account will automatically add £1000 pounds sterling worth of XAT units to your account, up to and including edition 21.**

Unlike pyramid schemes which promise everyone a huge and equal return, but soon run out of people to provide it, the XAT bonus offered actually goes down the later you leave it to join, so if you wait until we are shipping edition 20, you stand to gain only 1000 units on release of edition 21 and that is where it ends.

Also because the bonus offered is in XAT units which we credit to your account, there is no question as to our ability to pay it, and of course while the bonus offered does decrease with each new edition released, the number of people to trade with increases.

**The sooner you order,
the bigger your bonus**

Check our web site if you want to see which edition we are sending out today.

www.xat.org

XAT is also available to download for free from this site, but you must order 2 paperback copies for 2 friends if you wish to open a bonus account.

There is a helpful order form which you'll find at the end of this book

Those who joined while we were shipping edition one have a potential bonus of 20,000 pounds sterling worth of XAT units, and I can say for sure that they already have at least 1000 in their accounts if you are reading this from a book.

Because the bonus is calculated **from the edition number we are shipping** when you order and not from the edition you are reading at the time, there is no way for me to say what your bonus potential might be. If the book you are holding looks weathered and old, it is possible we are beyond edition 21 by now and your only bonus potential is to try and sell your copy to a collector.

Things are moving very fast as people realise this thing is really working, and because all it needs is lots of people with imagination and good will, it's not surprising that the XAT trading network is steadily growing and growing.

And of course **anyone with an account can decide how much or little they use it** so many people are investing the small amount needed on the chance that it might work, realising if it doesn't there is not much to lose. All account holders can claim to hold a share in the future where taxes could be a thing of the past.

After all, at the very worst, you get to send an interesting conversation piece to two of your friends, and if that is how you got your copy, you already know what a pleasant surprise it can be to know a friend selected you. It's meant to be fun with a purpose, and it is.

OF COURSE YOU'LL SPEND IT

Those who open XAT accounts whilst we're supplying early editions, will suddenly find they have a considerable sum in their account by the time edition 21 comes out. They will also have access to over a million people with buying power, and things to trade and sell.

Of course you will buy things and be able to sell things with this extra cash. Even on the simplest level, imagine you are on your way into a car boot sale and someone offers you a coupon which they say entitles you to buy £100 worth of goods. Of course you are going to spend it.

You are not going to turn it down if they say the coupon won't be honoured in Woolworths are you? No way. You'll spend it where it's valid because after all it is a bonus and you may as well cash it in cause it's no good to you sitting in your pocket. And that is what other people will do too, so you'll have no shortage of customers if it's something you want to sell. or a service you wish to offer.

We will keep you posted on what is being offered, and explain how you can sell things as well. As the numbers keep growing more and more people will see the value of XAT. You can keep track of what other XAT members are buying and selling by going to our website directory, which has just gone online and is waiting for your input to grow.

Once connected with this offer, it's all free.

MAKE IT OFFICIAL

There is no point in starting a journey if you don't have what it takes to finish. In this case we will have no problem expanding our up and running computer trading network to accommodate the needs of our growing membership. This really is an idea whose time has come.

Since edition one, a volunteer Core Maintenance Group has been set up to insure everything runs smoothly and everyone concerned has a say. The basic principles this is set up on, appear later in our Question Time section.

The statement being made by those who are joining is a clear signal that a new and fairer economic system is genuinely desired by many, but realistically we don't expect that current political parties would include this idea in their manifestoes, so once we have a large enough number of members, we could set up our own party and elect the concept in ourselves.

We could go one step further and use this amazing XAT network to allow each of us to vote on things over the phone or through the internet.

Real Democracy for the people by the people, minus politicians.

Even ten years ago this seemed like a futuristic idea waiting for the technology to make it possible, but today we already have what it takes to hold a secure vote using touch tone phones and encrypted software.

Initially we will be using this voting system to allow every XAT account holder to help guide the growing direction of XAT. This will allow us to properly test out our electronic voting system before we suggest it's wider use.

This basic idea of replacing parliament with an electronic voting system was presented to me over 15 years ago by a friend who suspects even the most original ideas have been thought of before. This positive option has been offered under a collection of colourful names at various elections and by-elections in the UK since that time.

His clever idea is that we have outgrown the need for politicians, and through the use of the technology we now possess, we could be provided with information, and allowed to voice our opinions on any issues which concern us through the process of **electronic voting**. He believes if we all held a common positive vision for our future, then we could guide ourselves there, without needing anyone else to represent us.

His personal vision sees a scenario within which the people of a London or Paris or New York or elsewhere declare themselves independent of any outside governance and become responsible for building a model city for the future from their collective dreams. What is your vision for the future? What chance does our present society provide for you to share your dream?

When the time comes and we are ready and in numbers, XAT along with other positive collectives could sponsor the deposits to allow enough candidates to run on **an electronic voting tax free platform.**

If this alternative attracted enough votes, it would replace the old one.

This is the only idea for a peaceful revolution I've ever been presented with. The current politicians and the current unjust system would simply have to stand down. No blood, no riots, it's beautiful. **Revolutionary democracy.**

To avoid confusion I should make it very clear that people running as candidates for such a Party would not be running to become leaders. They would be there to allow you to vote for yourself.

In the event that the election succeeded, parliament as it is now would be dissolved and you would be allowed to vote on issues which matter to you **through electronic voting,** providing a genuine democracy with government by referendum.

WE HAVE THE TECHNOLOGY, WE CAN REBUILD IT

Every television and radio programme dealing with social issues could take part in the process, plus new programmes could be created to cover some issues in detail. We already have many such programmes, some of which allow public phone votes already.

Newspaper and magazines could also help in providing information, and of course the internet would play a major part.

Instead of having the expert facts argued over by politicians with possible vested interests, we could consider the expert findings ourselves, and decide directly, cutting out the middle men and their extortionate fees. For example, if you wanted to know how best to deal with the problems faced by the NHS, wouldn't it better to take advice from the professionals within the service itself, rather than trusting the judgment of some rich politician in Westminster.

General maintenance, like rubbish collection, doesn't need to be voted for. Basic needs should be provided, not argued over.

Obviously not everyone would be interested in voting on every issue, but important issues would not be decided without giving you a chance to have your say. The obligation would be according to your conscience and what you felt was important to you. If it concerns you, then have a right to help decide its direction. If you would rather leave some things for others to decide, then you would have that option too.

Electronic voting can be done from almost anywhere. There's no need to spend hours travelling backwards and forwards to voting booths, and if a deadline was given for when votes needed to be cast, (allowing sufficient time to way up the pros and cons of each issue), you could conceivably vote, in a relaxed way as and when you pleased.

The whole process could become a natural part of our lives, with voting made easy with an XAT type network.

WHAT'S IMPORTANT TO YOU?

To help make this idea a reality and not just a good idea, XAT account holders are currently being invited to take part in phone vote opinion polls to test the network. If you would like to suggest any ideas for members to vote on, you can submit them in various convenient ways

1. email **vote4yourself@xat.org**

2. write to Vote4yourself, P.O. Box 10059. London NW2 6WR

3. See the form on our website http://www.xat.org

4. phone the special lines on the numbers you will receive in your account holder's pack

Account holders will obviously be notified that votes are taking place. You'll need to use your account number and PIN to vote so there is no double voting.

We are very fortunate to have the technology to make electronic voting possible and we intend to demonstrate that it can work well and be fun. With your help that will be no problem

The beauty of my friend's idea is that it provides an opportunity for all of us to present our ideas and to take part in deciding which ones we would like to see developed.

I've not mentioned his name here because this publication is absolutely full of suggested ideas and mentioning one contributor would be unfair to all the rest. Let me just say here, thank you all from us all!

History confirms, and economists agree, that XAT allowing us to live tax free, would work if we applied it. But because it is contrary to our current ideology, there is no way provided by the system for us to try it, and our only chance to develop an idea like this is to exploit this loophole which has been pointed out, and with our common sense, vote out the system.

Nothing to lose. We don't have democracy at the moment anyway, what we have is a voted in dictatorship.

With this token democracy they provide, we have no real say at all.

Have you considered that there is currently no way provided for the consideration of new ideas within our so called democracy?

With bankers and multinational corporations able to manipulate the economy, what difference does it make who we vote in? My observation is that it makes no real difference to us at all. After the last election, who can say they actually felt any personal difference?

At present our system rewards the politicians with loads of money and fancy cars, but what have they done for us lately? What new ideas have they proposed to make our lives better? When is the last time they spoke out over the built-in injustice that exists in their system?

People on the excess side of injustice don't usually complain.

By adopting a new economic method which is generous to all instead of just generous to a few, any country could set an example that would be followed by the rest of the world. And God knows the world needs to be freed from the money changers strangle.

In an effort to appear fair they tell us that anyone who wants to can stand for election, and then they go on to charge a small fortune for the privilege of being entered as candidate. For all their talk of fairness and equal opportunity, politics really is just a rich man's game. But together we can change all that. Through the use of electronic voting you could call in your vote and implement the use of XAT tax free money to provide genuine community needs, and from then on you would be allowed to keep everything you earn, and the natural good will you were created with could provide all the services your community requires.

LET THERE BE LIGHT

ONCE OFFICIAL, we could pay everyone's electricity and gas bill with money we produced in the same way that we provided for other services!

THE PRINCIPLES

XAT provides an exchange system which is independent and allows free trade.

At its lowest level it is a strong peaceful statement expressing dissatisfaction with the present financial system, allowing members to trade separately along side it.

At its highest level it suggests an alternative to peacefully replace the present system which could be democratically voted in.

Its objectives are genuinely peaceful and totally non violent.

Because of its unique computer network which can be accessed from any touch tone phone, XAT is capable of almost instantly knowing the opinion of it's members. When you are invited to vote on different issues, we hope you will take the time to make yourself heard.

We also hope you will use our web site to pose your own questions.

The results of polls taken using the XAT network may be made available for publication or disclosed to parties concerned in order to help encourage positive action in our world but your actual vote remains confidential, and your personal information will never be provided to anyone else.

XAT will not attempt to meddle in your personal life. It is not a cult and it remains neutral on personal faith issues.

It does not condone violence or destruction as a means to achieve any of it's peaceful objectives.

It is maintained to be of service to all it's members while respecting individual freedom.

Being a member does not require you to do anything after joining. You are invited to take part and trade as much or as little as you might wish.

LET BUSINESS JOIN IN

Once the numbers grow, there will no doubt be many businesses who will wish to have XAT accounts. This obviously won't happen in the early stages, but a business director becoming aware that there are, for instance, over a million people trading in an alternative currency will no doubt want to draw some of that crowd to his shop door. This may start by him simply offering to accept a small percentage of his goods price in XAT amounting to a discount for XAT members.

XAT account holders could become a very positive incentive for big business, encouraging ethical and responsible behaviour through various extra bonus schemes.

Our aim is to make this so good, and so attractive, that companies will be willing to rethink their approach for the chance to take part.

YOUR QUESTION TIME

Many questions have come in since the release of edition one along with some excellent suggestions. XAT is intended to be interactive and your input is vital to it's growth. The next few pages will be dedicated to your contributions and hopefully this section will grow as XAT does. Contributors to this section should be aware that no names are included here as often simular questions have come from various sources. You know who you are and we thank you for taking the time to contact us.

Q. How much is a unit in XAT worth when trading?

A. One unit should be valued at equal to one pound sterling or the local exchange unit of the country you are in which has an XAT trading network.

Q. How do I trade in XAT?

A. Providing you have units in your account, you can arrange for transfer of units to someone else's account simply by phoning the number we send you and following the instructions. You should have your account number and PIN ready to key in when requested to do so, (firmly and not too quickly to avoid mistakes).

Q. When I used my account recently I was unable to add 50p to the price I transferred. Why is this?

A. To speed up transactions and allow maximum use with minimum waiting, the current system as I write, does not deal in pence. This may change in the future if users feel the need for it. Meanwhile you should round your transactions to the nearest pound or local unit.

Q. Will I receive a balance statement?

A. No. You can simply call the XAT line and be instantly told your current balance by following the instructions you'll hear. You are also automatically told your new balance each time you trade in XAT units.

Q. What about forgery?

A. At present, XAT units exist electronically. There are no notes or coins which could be forged.

Q. What about computer hackers?

A. While XAT accounts are held on computer, access can only be gained through using touch tone phones. The XAT computer is completely isolated from other computers as it is not on the internet. All internet correspondence and backup transfers are done from a separate computer.

Q. How do you pronounce XAT?

A. Any way you like, it belongs to you.

Q. What does XAT stand for?

A. It's TAX backwards, as being the opposite to our current taxation system.

Q. Where is the XAT central computer kept?

A. In a jam jar under my bed. Actually it is a portable unit able to connect to a mobile phone network, and could at this moment be anywhere.

Q. What computer system does XAT use?

A. We would rather not tell you that for security reasons, but we can say it is a system on the same level as those used by major phone banking systems and is powered by Apple Mac.

Q. Could XAT overthrow the central banking system?

A. It could become the trading system of choice, and it could be elected official in any democratic country, but overthrow is not really the word I would use, as XAT is totally peaceful and non violent. How about "outshine the current system"?

Q. Will people joining in the United States have to call the UK computer to trade?

A. No. Separate accounting computers will be set up in each country the book is released in and sit along side that country's present currency. The exchange rate between countries will be equal to the current currency exchange rate to save confusion. XAT fits neatly on top of any present democratic system like an upgrade, until such time as it is voted in as the trading network of choice. You will be able to convert local XAT currency into foreign currency with a simple phone call, so XAT funds can be waiting for you when you travel abroad, providing the country you travel to has XAT members.

Q. Is anything deducted from my account for making transactions?

A. No, all transactions are free to all account holders.

Q. Can I get a bigger bonus by buying more than two copies of XAT for my friends?

A. Unfortunately not. The holding of more than one bonus account per person is not within the spirit of XAT and discouraged. Proof of ID may be required if someone is suspected of bonus hogging. There are however some competitions planned where you can earn bonus XAT units. Members will be notified of these. One suggestion is a phone-in radio competition where you send us a tape of you on a talk-in radio show, talking about XAT and we credit you a certain amount for each minute you stayed on the air. There might also be extra prizes for the most entertaining, and the longest call. We are also considering awarding extra points for letters about XAT which get printed in local and national papers.

And possibly simular prizes for unique publicity stunt ideas. Let us know if you have any.

Q. In XAT1 you say we should have 20,000 units by the time edition 20 comes out. I calculate this to be only 19,000. Please explain?

A. You're right. We have made a millennium type mistake here and you'll find to make up for it the bonus has been extended to include edition 21 in this edition, so the highest potential actually is 20,000 XAT units as we promised. Red faces all round and happy real millennium in 2001.

Q. I got my copy of XAT from a bookshop. Do I still have to get two copies for friends to get my bonus account?

A. Yes. No matter how you got your copy, from a bookshop, from a friend or free on the net, you must order your 2 copies for two friends (at the special low price) from **Those Publishers P.O. Box 10059 London NW2 6WR** to qualify for a bonus account, not forgetting to provide us with your address as well as theirs so we can send you your personal account details. (forms available on the net and in book editions)

Q. I've noticed there is some advertising in XAT. How is this set up?

A. If you are a bank like Lloyds TSB who bought the last page of edition one because they wanted to be in a book about the history of banking, it is very expensive. If you are a good cause like Jubilee 2000 and we have some extra space, it could be free.

Q. How about calling an XAT unit a "Wonder" 500 a "Blessing" 1000 a "Vision" and a million a "Miracle"?

A. Not a bad idea but I'll bet you a "Wonder" to two "Blessings" that we will receive other suggestions on this. Perhaps this is something we could all vote on. For the moment, for lack of a better name, we are trading in XATs.

Q. Did you know? In Southern Ireland there was a general bank strike in the early 1970's (or late1960's). As a result there was no access to currency of any official sort. The farming community issued personal cheques which were endorsed and used as cash, until cheque books ran out. After that people issued cheques written on anything from plain paper to cigarette packets, after the strike EVERYONE of these personal cheques were honoured.

A. No we didn't know. This is exactly the sort of thing we love to hear about.

Thank you very much for writing.

Many of you were expressing concern about the structure of XAT while others have suggested outlines to make sure it doesn't become like the thing it is designed to replace.

The following is made up from suggestions we received to really define the structure and workings of XAT. This is not written in stone and is open to further suggestions to improve it, so do contact us if you have any positive comments to make.

1. MISSION STATEMENT

To provide / offer humanity / a Model for an Economy / and a transaction system that promotes fair trade and exchange that is neutral, open and free from usury and vested interest and empowers individual and community value...

2. AIMS & OBJECTIVES

To promote awareness of the unfair basis of today's financial banking systems,

To implement a model for a local and global trade and exchange system that values the individual and supports the wealth of community skills and labour, and to make this available to be democratically elected as the trading method of choice when membership numbers are large enough to give it a chance of winning.

Such a model will be neutral and free from usury and taxation,

To provide an information service through which Members can exchange goods and services, and maintains a central account of transactions for the benefit of Members in each country the network is adopted.

3. MEMBERSHIP GUIDELINES - how to get the best of XAT

4. ACCOUNT HOLDERS AGREEMENT

Accepts XAT founding principles and tries to apply them to daily life, making a peaceful non violent statement expressing the desire for a fairer system of trade, simply by being an XAT account holder.

May be asked to show proof of identity when joining, such as a photo copy of ID, especially if there are multiple applications from the same address, (so as to avoid duplicate account holding)

Duplicating accounts is discouraged and will be cancelled if discovered.

PLUS

A. XAT is a non-profit membership society. It is maintained by the XAT Core Maintenance Group, who act on behalf of the members to maintain the accounting equipment and promote it's growth.

It is sponsored by 'Those Publishers' who are solely responsible for all of it's publications, publishing these independently, providing free XAT promotion and supplying, at no profit, copies of XAT sent by members to friends under the XAT bonus scheme. All excess from these transactions is dedicated to maintaining and promoting the XAT network.

B. XAT provides a free information service through which members can exchange goods and services, and maintains a central account of that exchange for the benefit of members.

C. Members agree to XAT holding their details on computer which is necessary to make transactions possible. XAT may use the details from time to time to inform members of bonus payouts, events or important developments. Literature from service providers may be included in mailouts from XAT with special arrangement, but personal details remain confidential and will not be provided to anyone.

D. Members may give or receive from one another credit in the XAT unit, called XAT (or a new name to be decided), providing they have sufficient balance in their accounts.

E. Only the account holder can authorise the transfer of units from their account to that of another's using the XAT phone system and their personal PIN. No other method is provided for transfer of funds.

F. No interest is charged or paid on accounts.

G. Bonus accounts automatically receive 1000 XAT units each time a new edition is issued after their joining date, up to and including edition 21.

Regular accounts start at 100 XATs, resulting from special free offers to be made from time to time at the sponsors discretion. The details concerning free offers may vary but will be made clear when the offer is made.

H. No old style money is deposited into or issued from XAT accounts. Members may engage in transactions entirely in XAT units, or on a part cash basis. But only XAT units are recorded on XAT accounts.

I. No-one is obliged to trade or vote on issues put forward and membership will not be affected by how much or little one participates.

J. XAT can give no warranty or undertaking as to the value, condition or quality of services or items offered. Members should seek to determine for themselves the quality or standard of workmanship offered before agreeing a purchase. XAT publishes a directory of resources and services made available by members but, as with any directory or newspaper, it cannot be held responsible for the quality of goods and services on offer.

K. Members are individually responsible for their own personal tax liabilities and returns. XAT has no liability to claims for tax on participants, and has no obligation or liability to report to the tax authorities or collect taxes on their behalf.

L. XAT administrators may decline to record an account or directory entry considered inappropriate for legal or other reasons.

M. Members have the right and are encouraged to attend any meeting of the Maintenance Group, and to participate in decision-making through the phone voting service provided. Members have the right of appeal on all maintenance decisions and such appeals should be made initially in writing by post or e-mail.

N. The Maintenance Group reserve the right to deny membership in exceptional circumstances at their discretion. The Maintenance group may act on behalf of the membership in seeking explanation or satisfaction from a person whose activity is considered to be contrary to the interests of the membership.

O. Members agree to be bound by the conditions of this Agreement.

The above should hopefully help to answer the bulk of questions we have received.

Once we begin to see that things need not stay the way they are, we really can begin to make things different.

The limits we now have are limits we have set on ourselves, or been conned into believing..

Once a man was watching a game of golf for the first time and he wondered what it was all about.

When he asked, no one could be bothered to explain it to him because it seemed so obvious to them. Finally one woman being literally Teed off by what seemed like silly questions said to this man "you have a ball and you have 18 holes in the grass and the object of the game is to get the ball into all the holes".

That evening our novice to golf got himself a ball, walked around the course and neatly put the ball into each hole by hand.

That was easy, he thought to himself, and he wondered what all the fuss was about.

The point is he had not limited himself to using golf clubs, and that made it easy for him to reach his goal each time without problem.

If we limit ourselves to an economic plan that is full of obstructions and requires us all to pay taxes, then to us that will seem as normal as it seems for Nick Faldo to swing a club, but if we all decide we would like to get from A to B in a smoother way, then that is up to us and very possible.

Personally I find our present economic system far too destructive to take it seriously as a thing of the future.

GET A SHARE IN THE FUTURE

This positive new plan is based on the idea that all those involved in it should benefit from it.

Even it's introduction is designed to benefit those who are quick off the mark to help establish it.

Each person who took up this offer while we were supplying edition one now has an extra 1000 units in their account. They stand to earn a maximum of 20,000 units with the bonus scheme. This being edition TWO as I write, you stand to gain 19,000 maximum, until that goes down on the release of edition THREE.

We told early readers that the only way they could really see if this will work was to try it.

It is working for them and it can work for you.

If we want something better, then we have to start somewhere. Why not here?

To open your XAT account all you need to do is order two paperback copies of the book you are holding for two friends at the special low price of £3.50 each; (XAT retails in paperback at £4.95).

100% of the profit made on your order will go towards maintaining and promoting the XAT network.

To take part you can use the order form you'll find on the next page

Now it's up to you.

**Please Don't Delay
Order Today!**

Give me a share in the furure.   Time for me ro get connected to XAT.

With No Obligation to Trade

my name and address are

Please open my BONUS Account with XAT

Name _____

Address _____

_____

_____ Post Code

e-mail (optional but desirable) _____

My two freinds whose addresses are below get paperback copies of XAT,
and I get my account with, PIN Number regular updates and use of directories

1st Friend's Name _____

Address _____

_____

_____ Post Code

Outside the UK please add £2.00 or equivalent for postage

I enclose £7.00 cheque or postal order

Send to: Those Publishers P.O.Box 10059 London NW2 6WR

2nd Friend's Name _____

Address _____

_____

_____

_____ Post Code

Please Print Clearly, These are your Address Labels

This form can be photocopied to save ruining the book.

JUBILEE 2000 COALITION

A debt-free start for a billion people

7 million children die each year
from preventable diseases
because their governments are sending money to
western bankers - instead of spending it on
their own people.

**1,625,969 people have died
in the first 3 months of the year 2000.**

Concerned?
Want to know more?
visit our website @

www.jubilee2000uk.org

**or write to:
Jubilee 2000 Coalition,
PO Box 100, London, SE1 7RT**